PLAYS BY EDWIN SÁNCHEZ

BROADWAY PLAY PUBLISHING INC
56 E 81st St., NY NY 10028-0202
212 772-8334 fax 212 772-8358

PLAYS BY EDWIN SÁNCHEZ

First printing: February 1997
ISBN: 0-88145-129-0

Book design: Marie Donovan
Word processing: Microsoft Word for Windows
Typographic controls: Xerox Ventura Publisher 2.0 PE
Typeface: Palatino
Printed on recycled acid-free paper and bound in the USA.

CONTENTS

ABOUT THE AUTHOR

Productions include UNMERCIFUL GOOD FORTUNE (A T & T On Stage New Play Award), co-produced by Northlight Theater and Victory Gardens in Chicago; CLEAN (Kennedy Center's Fund for New American Plays, nominated by the American Theater Critics Association as Best New Play 1995) produced by Hartford Stage; TRAFFICKING IN BROKEN HEARTS at the Atlantic Theater Company in New York; FLOORSHOW: DOÑA SOL AND HER TRAINED DOG at Latino Chicago; and FATTY TISSUE, produced by Theater by Design of Chicago. His work has been workshopped at the Mark Taper Forum, Seattle Rrepertory Company, and South Coast Repertory, for whom he is currently commissioned to write a new play.

He is the recipient of a 1995 Berrilla Kerr Foundation Award, the 1994 Princess Grace Playwriting Award, the 1994 ASCAP Cole Porter Award, the 1993 Barrie Stavis Playwriting Fellowship, the 1993 Eugene O'Neill Scholarship, the 1992 George Pierce Baker Scholarship, the 1991 William Morris Agency Fellowship, and a 1989 Artists Fellowship in Playwriting presented by the New York State Arts Council. He participated in 1995's Sundance Screenwriting Lab and is a 1994 graduate of the Yale School of Drama. Mr Sánchez is a member of the Dramatists Guild and New Dramatists.

CLEAN

ORIGINAL PRODUCTION

CLEAN premiered at The Hartford Stage (Mark Lamos, Artistic Director; Stephen Albert, Managing Director) on 25 March 1995. The cast and creative contributors were:

GUSTAVITO . . . . Joe Quintero
MERCY . . . . Paula Pizzi
KIKO . . . . Mateo Gomez
FATHER . . . . Neil Maffin
JUNIOR . . . . Nelson Vasquez
NORRY . . . . A Benard Cummings

Director . . . . Graciela Daniele
Set design . . . . Christopher Barreca
Costume design . . . . Eduardo Sicangco
Light design . . . . David F Segal
Sound design . . . . David Budries
Original music . . . . Robert C Cotnoir
Production dramaturg . . . . Kim Euell
Casting . . . . Bernard Telsey Casting
Production stage manager . . . . Barbara Reo
Assistant stage manager . . . . Deborah Vandergrift

This play was originally produced with the assistance of the Fund for New American Plays, a project of the John F Kennedy Center for the Performing Arts, with support from American Express Company in cooperation with the President's Committee on the Arts and Humanities.

CHARACTERS

FATHER
MERCY
KIKO
JUNIOR
GUSTAVITO
NORRY

GUSTAVITO *is 7 and* JUNIOR *is 12 at the beginning of the play. The action takes place during the course of eight years.*

The first act takes place in the Bronx, NY. The second act takes place in the Bronx and Puerto Rico.

ACT ONE

(The stage is dark. A giant cross begins to glow. It takes up most of the stage and is located in the center. One key of music is heard; the cross rises. Standing behind the brilliant, white cross is GUSTAVITO*, age 7, played by an adult actor and wearing only his jockey shorts. He runs to the edge of the stage. He is the only figure we see in a pool of light.)*

GUSTAVITO: *(Sings)*
Two and time
follow me
to the bottom of the sea.
While you're there
wash your hair
and your dirty underwear.

MERCY: *(Voice only)* Gustavito, you had better get yourself—

GUSTAVITO *(Sings)*	MERCY
Two and time	—into this bath tub.
follow me	
to the bottom of the sea.	
While you're there	
wash your hair	I'm not kidding with
and your dirty underwear.	you.

(The lights come up to reveal a small bathroom. MERCY *is kneeling by the bath tub.* GUSTAVITO *gets into the bath tub, still wearing his underwear.)*

MERCY: My dirty, little man.

(She begins to bathe him.)

GUSTAVITO: Mercy, don't touch my thing.

MERCY: Nobody want to touch that dirty thing. It smells. *(She puts her hand in the water and grabs him, takes out her hand and smells it.)* Oooh, stinky.

GUSTAVITO: Nah-uh.

(She kisses the top of his head.)

MERCY: Mercy's dirty, little boy.

(The sound of a door opening and closing is heard. KIKO *has arrived.)*

KIKO: *(Voice only)* Mercedes!

*(*MERCY *locks the bathroom door. She takes a hammer, which has been sitting on the toilet seat, and holds it in her hand.)*

KIKO: Mercedes! Can't you hear your Kiko calling you?

*(*GUSTAVITO *goes underwater.)*

MERCY: Gustavito. Gustavito.

*(*GUSTAVITO *emerges.)*

GUSTAVITO: Is Kiko mad?

MERCY: Take off your underwear, no he's not mad, and wash it. Like this.

(She puts the hammer on her lap and mimes washing clothing by rubbing her fists against each other. KIKO *begins to bang against the door.* MERCY *flinches, but continues.)*

KIKO: Goddamn it, I gotta take a shit, Mercedes!

*(*MERCY *picks up the hammer. She takes out a magazine and begins to look through it.)*

MERCY: I'll make you a nice birthday cake and we'll put seven candles on it, with one for luck. Two and time, follow me... Come on, Gustavito.

*(*GUSTAVITO *softly sings his song.)*

KIKO: Open the fucking door, Mercedes! *(He begins to pound on the door.* MERCY *puts the magazine down and stands by attention at the door, hammer poised in mid-air.)* Mercedes!

MERCY: To the bottom of the sea.

*(*GUSTAVITO *begins to wash his underwear.)*

GUSTAVITO: While you're there wash your hair and your dirty underwear. I'm scared.

MERCY: If he really wanted to get in he would.

KIKO: *(Softly)* Mercedes.

GUSTAVITO: While you're there—

MERCY: All he has to do is turn the knob.

GUSTAVITO: —wash your hair...big bubble.

(He hums the rest of the song. MERCY *is lovingly tracing a heart on the door with the hammer. The sudden silence brings her from her reverie. She tries to get* GUSTAVITO *singing again.)*

MERCY: And your dirty.

GUSTAVITO: Un-der-wear.

(A church confessional. GUSTAVITO *enters and takes a seat in the penitent's side. He is wearing a baseball cap.)*

GUSTAVITO: Forgive me Father, for I have sinned. This is my first confession.

FATHER: Yes, go ahead my son.

GUSTAVITO: I stole a hat, a baseball cap.

FATHER: From where?

GUSTAVITO: From Woolworth's.

FATHER: You have to take it back.

GUSTAVITO: I can't. *(He takes off the cap.)* I lost it.

FATHER: Forgiveness will only come if you pay for your sins.

GUSTAVITO: I'm real sorry. I don't have any money. They dared me to do it.

FATHER: Who did?

GUSTAVITO: Some friends.

FATHER: Those aren't your friends.

GUSTAVITO: I can get the money from Mercy.

FATHER: She wasn't the one who stole it.

GUSTAVITO: I won't do it again.

FATHER: What did you do with the hat?

GUSTAVITO: I didn't even want it. I was so scared I just threw it away. Sister Frances at school, she started telling us about Hell and how terrible it is. I don't want to go there. Help me, please.

FATHER: I want you to say three Our Fathers and think about what you did. Will you promise me you'll never steal again?

GUSTAVITO: Uh-huh. Can you see me?

FATHER: What?

GUSTAVITO: Can you see me? I can't see you.

*(*FATHER *crosses himself. Lights down.)*

*(*KIKO *is asleep in his armchair. He is snoring loudly.* MERCY *and* GUSTAVITO *enter.* GUSTAVITO *sits at* KIKO*'s feet and very tenderly and slowly removes* KIKO*'s shoes and socks through the course the scene.)*

MERCY: *(Almost to herself.)* I don't know when I'm going, but I'm going.

GUSTAVITO: He gets corns on his feet. They're very rough. He must have walked barefoot a lot.

MERCY: He was barefoot when I first met him. Pant legs rolled up, in the river behind our house. Consuelo and me, we first saw him together.

GUSTAVITO: I've seen him cut off the corns with a razor. He draws blood sometimes. He wanted to teach me how to do it, but I hid. No way.

MERCY: *(Sweetly)* Pendejo.

GUSTAVITO: Pendeja tu.

MERCY: Do you miss your mother? Just now, that little pout reminded me of her.

GUSTAVITO: I don't remember her.

MERCY: Esperanza wasn't even with us when we saw Kiko. What a shameless man. To marry all three sisters. And when he came for me, I was going to be different. I was going to stand in that doorway and chase him away. Instead, I had my bag packed the night before. Maybe he was the price the Gomez sisters had to pay to leave their family. I'll tell you a little secret. You were supposed to be mine. Kiko married Consuelo first, although for a long time I don't think he knew which one he liked better. Then, he chose Esperanza. I came in a very distant third.

GUSTAVITO: It wasn't a contest, Mercy.

MERCY: Oh yes it was. Consuelo got him then Esperanza got him and I got to take care of my parents. And do you know, when Consuelo passed on—

GUSTAVITO: Died.

MERCY: —went to Heaven, and Esperanza escaped to God-knows-where, Kiko comes with his hat in his hand to see if I'm available. If I'm available.

GUSTAVITO: You were waiting for him.

MERCY: To punish him. *(She mimes locking her lips with a key.)* We have been together for seven years and I have never let him touch me. And he won't.

GUSTAVITO: Don't you want him to touch you?

MERCY: Give me his socks, I'll wash them.

GUSTAVITO: That's my job. I wear them like gloves and let the water run and wash my hands.

MERCY: You leave too much soap in them.

GUSTAVITO: I do not. *(Pause)* Don't you want him to touch you?

*(*MERCY *exits.* GUSTAVITO *remains crouched at* KIKO*'s feet.)*

GUSTAVITO: So today at school we had a spelling bee and I won so I got a star by my name. A star means I'm good.

*(*KIKO *snores as he changes positions.)*

GUSTAVITO: And Jose Manuel wanted to wait outside for me and beat me up 'cause he said I was showing off. I told him you would come in and beat him up if he did....I stole something today.

(In the now-empty church, GUSTAVITO *approaches* FATHER.*)*

GUSTAVITO: Father. I waited for you.

*(*FATHER *looks at him quizzically.)*

GUSTAVITO: I'm the one who stole the baseball cap.

FATHER: Ah. You were here with your mother. Where is she?

GUSTAVITO: She's not my mother. She's Mercy. She don't like going to church so she always crochets. She's going to go to Hell, right, Father?

FATHER: That's not exactly how it works. So, did you tell your father what you did?

GUSTAVITO: Oh, he forgave me. That was a nice Mass you did. How old were you when you knew you wanted to be a priest?

FATHER: About your age I guess.

GUSTAVITO: Who did you tell?

FATHER: My parents.

GUSTAVITO: Were they proud that God had chosen you?

FATHER: God didn't choose me, I chose Him.

GUSTAVITO: Same thing.

FATHER: *(Sharply)* No, there's a very big difference.

GUSTAVITO: Okay, okay, there's a very big difference. I bet I can tell you what you were like at my age.

FATHER: Bet you can't.

GUSTAVITO: You were a lot like me, I think I'm more curiouser, though.

FATHER: Curious. Do you have a lot of friends?

GUSTAVITO: No, not really. Uh, no.

FATHER: Maybe you are like me at your age.

GUSTAVITO: A priest job would be perfect for me. What do you do all day? Pray and listen to secrets.

FATHER: They're not secrets, they're sins. I'll tell you what, I'll bring you a little book next week, okay?

GUSTAVITO: For me?

FATHER: Yeah, for you. You see another thief around here? *(He pulls the baseball cap from* GUSTAVITO*'s back pocket.)* I'm kidding.

GUSTAVITO: But not about the book, right?

FATHER: No, not about the book.

GUSTAVITO: I'll see you next week then.

*(*GUSTAVITO *runs out. He has left the baseball cap behind.)*

(The Delgado living room)

KIKO: Te voy a decir la purisima verdad. I am going to tell you the purest of truths. "Purest of truths". Not diluted by lies, not even a little bit. *(He shuffles a deck of cards and quickly sets out the cards for a game of solitaire. He speeds through the deck, to hurry along the game. His game is not about rules, it is about speed.)*

JUNIOR: Anytime today.

KIKO: God invented love to punish people.

JUNIOR: Good night.

*(*KIKO *has gone as far as he can with this game. He collects the cards and shuffles them as before and begins again.)*

KIKO: You see Mercy? I love Mercy. Don't I, honey?

*(*MERCY *does not look up from her sewing.)*

MERCY: The word loses all value in your mouth.

KIKO: *(To* JUNIOR*)* And I loved your mother, Consuelo. *(To* GUSTAVITO And I even had enough love left over to love your mother, Gustavito.

GUSTAVITO: Mami Esperanza.

KIKO: You know I'm talking to you 'cause I care.

JUNIOR: He's drunk out of his mind.

KIKO: I would rather be in love than anything.

GUSTAVITO: And if they don't love you back?

KIKO: All the better. Right, Mercy?

*(*MERCY *ignores him.)*

KIKO: Right.

JUNIOR: Shit, a woman don't know I love her I make her know.

*(*MERCY *gives him a condescending look.)*

JUNIOR: It's the truth. *(To* GUSTAVITO, *referring to* KIKO*)* Weak man.

KIKO: *(Referring to his game)* A spade is a spade.

JUNIOR: Don't know how to carry his balls. Hope you didn't turn out the same way. If you love somebody, they belong to you. Period. That's how it is. You see Mercy? She belong to Kiko.

GUSTAVITO: You full of shit.

*(*KIKO *takes his card table to* MERCY *so that she can see his game. She does not look up.* KIKO *exits.* JUNIOR *takes* GUSTAVITO*'s middle finger and folds it back.* GUSTAVITO *winces in pain.)*

JUNIOR: Shut up so you can hear the sound of the bone breaking.

GUSTAVITO: Mercy.

*(*MERCY *looks up.)*

JUNIOR: *(Under his breath)* Crack.

*(*GUSTAVITO *is silent.* MERCY *exits.)*

JUNIOR: Who's full of shit?

GUSTAVITO: I am.

JUNIOR: And who's not?

GUSTAVITO: You.

JUNIOR: You're gonna be just like Kiko. The ball-less wonder. *(He exits.)*

*(*GUSTAVITO *gets on his knees in prayer. Lights dim so that only a dim light remains on him. Lights slowly begin to come up as* KIKO *enters, dressed for work and with his lunch pail. He looks at* GUSTAVITO, *shakes his head, and exits. Lights slowly come up to full. A knock is heard.* MERCY *enters in a disheveled house dress and her hair uncombed.)*

GUSTAVITO: Amen. *(Crossing himself and running to the door.)*

MERCY: Don't you dare open that door, Gustavito.

*(*GUSTAVITO *opens the door to reveal* NORRY, *who is wearing an evening dress. He is in full make-up.)*

GUSTAVITO: Uyy. *(He runs and hides behind* MERCY.*)*

NORRY: Aren't you just the cutest little thing?

*(*GUSTAVITO *shakes his head from behind* MERCY.*)*

NORRY: Well, suit yourself. *(To* MERCY*)* Mercedes La Milagrosa?

MERCY: Yes. *(She tries to make herself more presentable.)*

NORRY: You're the seamstress who can do anything, huh?

MERCY: Yes. I'm sorry, come in.

(NORRY enters)

GUSTAVITO: *(To MERCY)* He's pretty.

MERCY: Sssh.

NORRY: No baby, I'm beautiful. My imitators are pretty. I want to hire you, Mercy.

MERCY: Call me Mercy.

NORRY: Money is no object as long as it doesn't cost more that a hundred dollars.

MERCY: I...I make dresses for women.

NORRY: I want a wedding dress.

MERCY: I don't think so.

NORRY: A mother fucking kind of wedding dress. *(He sits in one, sweeping, graceful movement.)* Do you have any coffee?

MERCY: No.

NORRY: A Puerto Rican house without coffee? Rebel.

MERCY: *(Smiles)* Gustavito, get lost.

NORRY: Comadre.

(GUSTAVITO pretends to leave, but hides behind a chair.)

NORRY: I'm thinking of something with lots of low cut, you know what I'm saying? Tight here *(Points to breasts)* and tight here *(Waist)* and Honey, very tight here. *(Hips)*

MERCY: This is a wedding dress?

NORRY: This is Norry's wedding dress.

MERCY: Well, Norry, I don't think my husband is going to like you here.

NORRY: And you always do what he says.

MERCY: You'd have to be here for fittings.

NORRY: I've been collecting white things to sew on this dress. Since forever.

MERCY: And Junior won't like it.

NORRY: It's for an act I do at the Red Castle. Nice little dive where my reign as Queen Bee is being threatened by a bunch of back-stabbing bitches who just recently lost the training wheels on their spike heels.

MERCY: English or Spanish, but this I don't understand.

(Enter JUNIOR. MERCY *rises, sensing trouble ahead.)*

MERCY: Uh, Junior, I need you to go to the store for me.

JUNIOR: Send the midget.

*(*NORRY *reaches into his purse and gives* JUNIOR *some money.)*

NORRY: Get me a beer and get yourself one, too.

*(*JUNIOR *is about to take the money. He stops and eyes* NORRY.*)*

JUNIOR: Hey, wait a second. You ain't no woman.

NORRY: It's okay. You're not a man, yet.

MERCY: Uh, Norry.

JUNIOR: Get your faggot ass outta this house. Now. Ahora.

NORRY: *(Dismissing* JUNIOR *and turning his attention to* MERCY*)* And I figured before the wedding dress we would do a showgirl outfit. Very Ann Margret. Right?

*(*JUNIOR *grabs* NORRY*'s arm and yanks him up.)*

JUNIOR: You're fucked.

NORRY: Okay, Papito, but you had better be ready to kill me 'cause with whatever you leave I will scrape it together and cut your cojones off and wear them for earrings.

*(*JUNIOR *pushes* NORRY, *who kicks off his heels.* MERCY *gets between them.)*

MERCY: Hey, hey, hey, hey.

NORRY: Let the boy try. As a man or as a woman I am too too much for him.

*(*KIKO *enters.* GUSTAVITO *peeks over from behind the chair and crosses himself.)*

KIKO: Mercy. *(To* NORRY*)* Doñita. I wasn't expecting company.

NORRY: Norry. Norry Del Alma.

MERCY: She wants me to sew for her.

KIKO: Your humble servant.

JUNIOR: Hello? It's a man in a dress. Hello?

*(*KIKO *slaps* JUNIOR.*)*

KIKO: In this house we respect our guests. He is wearing a dress so in this house he's a she. *(He takes off his belt and folds in menacingly.)* You understand me?

*(*JUNIOR *makes a blustery show of heading to the door.)*

JUNIOR: Let me see if I can invite more freaks into this fucking house.

(KIKO slams him against the wall. He takes him by the hair and slams his head against the wall.)

MERCY: Kiko, por favor.

KIKO: The question, "You understand me?"

JUNIOR: Yeah.

(KIKO lets him go.)

KIKO: Go out for an hour.

(JUNIOR exits, looking down at the floor.)

MERCY: One of these days you're gonna hurt that boy, Kiko. I think that's why he's crazy.

KIKO: Don't worry. I'll beat the craziness out of him.

(NORRY looks from KIKO to MERCY.)

NORRY: *(Awkwardly)* I seem to be barefoot.

(KIKO offers his arm as NORRY gets back in his heels.)

MERCY: So you were saying showgirl, right?

NORRY: Huh?

MERCY: You'll want a head dress.

NORRY: Yeah. To the sky. Or so I can wear it on the subway.

MERCY: I've never made a head dress before.

NORRY: I'll help you.

KIKO: Mercy, have you offered our guest any refreshment?

MERCY: I'm the hostess! I know when I have to offer stuff! *(To NORRY)* You want some Tang?

KIKO: Go make some Tang for us.

NORRY: Just a little bit. That would be nice, yeah.

(MERCY exits)

KIKO: Gustavito, come on, stop hiding. Everybody's seen you already. Take off my shoes.

(GUSTAVITO emerges from his hiding place and begins to take off KIKO's shoes.)

NORRY: You must be on your feet all day, huh? My father was a, was a, was a waiter so he was always on his feet. What do you do, Don Kiko?

(KIKO motions NORRY to lean in.)

KIKO: In my house, my family is sacred. You don't disrespect me or my family.

NORRY: I would never do that.

(KIKO holds up his hand to silence NORRY.)

KIKO: Outside of this house you can set fire to yourself for all I care, but here, no. You don't come here when my children are here and you are only allowed to sit in the living room. You don't cross that doorway. *(Points to doorway leading to the rest of the apartment)* You want Mercy to sew for you, okay. But you remember, you have no friends here.

(The Rectory. GUSTAVITO is showing the FATHER pictures. The first is of the Delgado men in their Sunday best.)

GUSTAVITO: This is Kiko and my brother Junior. *(The next shot is of KIKO and JUNIOR. They both have beers in their hands.)* Junior's not supposed to drink yet, but... *(The next shot is of MERCY and GUSTAVITO.)* This is Mercy and me.

FATHER: She your mother?

GUSTAVITO: No.

FATHER: Is she Junior's mother?

GUSTAVITO: No.

(The next shot is of KIKO and MERCY. They appear ill at ease.)

GUSTAVITO: This is Kiko and Mercy.

FATHER: Is she your father's sister?

GUSTAVITO: No, she's his wife. They just don't like each other.

(The next shot is of MERCY. She is alone and is wearing a cocktail dress. Her hair and make-up are done and she looks seductively into the camera.)

GUSTAVITO: I'm not supposed to show that one. All the rest are like that. Pretty shots. She likes that. Kinda sexy.

FATHER: You have a very handsome family.

GUSTAVITO: Yeah. Thank you, I mean. Here.

(He gives him a picture.)

GUSTAVITO: That's me. You can keep it.

FATHER: No, I can't do that. They belong to your family.

GUSTAVITO: It's okay. I'll tell them I lost it.

(FATHER playfully hits him on the head with the picture.)

FATHER: You're not supposed to lie, remember.

GUSTAVITO: They won't mind I gave it to you.

(FATHER looks at the picture once again.)

FATHER: You'll let me know if they want it back?

(GUSTAVITO nods. Silence.)

GUSTAVITO: Do you think Mercy's pretty?

FATHER: Yes, she's very pretty.

(GUSTAVITO tries to imitate one of MERCY's poses.)

GUSTAVITO: Do you think we look alike?

FATHER: ...No.

GUSTAVITO: I do. Thank you again for the book.

FATHER: Now you read it, okay?

GUSTAVITO: Yeah. You're real nice, you know.

FATHER: Just doing my job.

GUSTAVITO: Oh.

FATHER: I'll see you in Mass.

GUSTAVITO: Is it okay if I come to visit you?

FATHER: Sure.

GUSTAVITO: Do you want me to come and visit you? I gotta go. Can I have a picture of you? Bring it tomorrow, okay.

(He runs out. JUNIOR is waiting for him outside.)

JUNIOR: You get lost in there?

GUSTAVITO: Sorry. *(He starts looking through his book.)*

JUNIOR: What's that?

GUSTAVITO: A book. The Father gave it to me.

JUNIOR: Why would he give you anything?

GUSTAVITO: I gave him a picture of me. We sorta traded. He likes me. A lot.

(JUNIOR stops him.)

JUNIOR: Go get the picture back—

GUSTAVITO: I'm not gonna (do that)

JUNIOR: —and give him back his book.

GUSTAVITO: No.

(JUNIOR *takes the book from* GUSTAVITO, *who begins to hit him.)*

GUSTAVITO: Give it back to me.

*(*JUNIOR *throws the book on the floor.)*

GUSTAVITO: Mother fucker.

*(*GUSTAVITO *tries to go for the book but* JUNIOR *twists* GUSTAVITO*'s arm behind his back.)*

GUSTAVITO: I'm gonna tell Kiko.

JUNIOR: Yeah, tell him so he can come down to the church and kill the priest. *(He kisses* GUSTAVITO*'s head, even as he holds his arm.)* If Kiko starts thinking there's something wrong he'll kill you, Gustavito. I'm not bullshitting. And ain't Mercy or me gonna be able to stop him.

GUSTAVITO: I didn't do nothing.

JUNIOR: Did the Father do anything to you?

GUSTAVITO: No, asshole.

*(*JUNIOR *twists his arm again.)*

GUSTAVITO: Ow, no, Junior.

JUNIOR: Promise me you'll never come here again. Promise.

GUSTAVITO: Break the mother fucking arm.

*(*JUNIOR *pushes* GUSTAVITO *away.* GUSTAVITO *picks up the book.)*

JUNIOR: I'm gonna give you a head start, then I'm gonna take that book and throw it away.

*(*GUSTAVITO *runs off.* FATHER *is getting into his car.* JUNIOR *surprises him and gets in on the passenger side. He has an unlit cigarette behind his ear.)*

JUNIOR: Yo, Padre.

*(*FATHER *stares at him for a moment.)*

JUNIOR: Going for a little ride? Good. I'm in the mood to travel. Put it in gear.

FATHER: Get out of the car.

JUNIOR: You know, even if you're parking on church property you should lock this baby up. People like to take what don't belong to them sometimes.

FATHER: Then I'm getting out.

*(*FATHER *tries to leave;* JUNIOR *grabs his arm.)*

JUNIOR: I'm paying you a visit, Father.

FATHER: I don't think so.

JUNIOR: Then consider this my confession. I think I want to kill you.

(FATHER *looks at* JUNIOR.)

JUNIOR: And that's a sin. But touching Gustavito is a sin, too. Isn't it?

(FATHER *swallows.)*

JUNIOR: I'm not getting an answer here. Hello? It's a sin, isn't it? *(Silence)* Have you touched him?

FATHER: *(Softly)* No.

JUNIOR: But you want to.

FATHER: I have never touched your brother.

JUNIOR: Well, I hope so for your sake. 'Cause I will kill you and this is not a threat, this is a fact. You hear what I'm saying?

(FATHER *nods.)*

JUNIOR: I don't think you should see him again. I don't think your filthy eyes should ever gaze on my little brother again. *(He puts his cigarette in his mouth and pushes in the car cigarette lighter. Silence.)*

FATHER: He likes to come to the church.

JUNIOR: *(Cutting him off)* —because you are scum.

(Silence. The lighter pops up and JUNIOR *lights his cigarette. He holds the lighter for a second and then holds it inches away from the* FATHER*'s face.* FATHER *is taken by surprise; he tries to move away but is trapped in the car.)*

JUNIOR: You would still have another eye. My brother ain't no faggot. My brother ain't never gonna be no faggot and if you make him one you'll have to deal with me. And I ain't God, I don't forgive. *(He puts the lighter back.)* So what's my penance?

FATHER: An act of kindness. That's all it was. Something I would have done for any child.

JUNIOR: Three hail Marys and all is forgiven? Thank you, Father. *(He gets out of the car.)*

FATHER: You're very wrong. I don't have any feelings for your brother.

*(*JUNIOR *exits.* FATHER *sits motionless for a second. He opens the car door and vomits.)*

(Living room. GUSTAVITO *lays out a towel on the sofa and sits next to it. The wedding dress on the sewing dummy is in its earliest stages.* MERCY *is hard at work on it.)*

KIKO: *(Referring to the towel)* What's that for?

GUSTAVITO: This is for God to sit.

KIKO: What he say?

MERCY: Leave him alone. He thinks God is sitting next to him.

KIKO: Saint Gustavito, huh?

MERCY: He goes to church every day.

JUNIOR: What do you do there all the time?

*(*GUSTAVITO *holds up his hand to stop him. He finishes praying.)*

GUSTAVITO: I pray.

JUNIOR: You're just a kid, what the fuck do you have to pray about?

*(*KIKO *gets up. It should appear that he is about to hit* JUNIOR.*)*

JUNIOR: What do you have to pray about. That's what I meant to say.

MERCY: Kiko, please.

JUNIOR: Quit hanging out in church, Gustavito. It looks bad.

*(*KIKO *exits into the kitchen.)*

MERCY: You got a filthy mind.

*(*KIKO *enters with a grater. He places it on the floor.)*

KIKO: *(To* JUNIOR*)* Kneel on it.

*(*MERCY *puts down her sewing.* GUSTAVITO *goes back to praying.* JUNIOR *slowly rises and is about to kneel on the grater.)*

KIKO: Lower your pants. Bare knees.

*(*JUNIOR *does. He kneels on the grater.)*

MERCY: This is why Esperanza left, Kiko.

KIKO: Nobody's holding you here. You leave today, I'll have somebody else tomorrow. *(To* JUNIOR*)* You stay there until midnight.

*(*KIKO *and* MERCY *exit.* GUSTAVITO*'s prayer slowly becomes louder. For the last line he is joined by* JUNIOR.*)*

JUNIOR & GUSTAVITO: ...now in the hour of our death, amen.

*(*GUSTAVITO *rises and enters the confessional.)*

GUSTAVITO: Forgive me Father, for I have sinned. It's me, Gustavito.

FATHER: You've got to be careful when you come here.

GUSTAVITO: I know, Junior. He's like watching me all the time. Asshole.

FATHER: What did you tell him?

GUSTAVITO: I didn't tell him nothing.

FATHER: Don't get into any trouble because of me.

GUSTAVITO: Hey, he's not my father. He's not you.

FATHER: Gustavito, I'm not your father.

GUSTAVITO: You're better than my father. I don't have to be afraid of you.

FATHER: You love Kiko, right?

GUSTAVITO: ...Yeah.

FATHER: He loves you very much.

GUSTAVITO: How do you know?

FATHER: Put your palm on the screen.

*(*GUSTAVITO *places his palm against the* FATHER*'s.)*

FATHER: I'm going to close my eyes, you close yours.

GUSTAVITO: Okay. Now what?

FATHER: I'll tell you a secret. Nobody can see us in here.

GUSTAVITO: I know that. That ain't no secret.

FATHER: No, I mean, you can't see me and I really can't see you. We're together, we're touching, but we can't see each other.

GUSTAVITO: Are you ashamed of me?

FATHER: No. Don't ever think that.

GUSTAVITO: Clap your hand against mine.

(They clap palms.)

GUSTAVITO: Make a wish. *(He exits confessional.)*

FATHER: I wish I were you.

GUSTAVITO: Can I try on your rosary?

FATHER: It's not a toy.

GUSTAVITO: That's okay. I'm not playing.

*(*FATHER *hesitates, begins to remove his rosary.)*

GUSTAVITO: What does it mean when you dream about somebody?

*(*FATHER *stops.)*

FATHER: What did you dream of?

GUSTAVITO: God. He was just floating there. Not saying anything. No expression on His face. But if I squinted my eyes—rosary, Father—

(FATHER *removes his rosary and holds it over* GUSTAVITO*'s head.)*

GUSTAVITO: —if I squinted my eyes I could pretend He was smiling.

(FATHER *is about to place the rosary around* GUSTAVITO*'s neck.)*

GUSTAVITO: Hold it a second. *(He pulls out his shirt tails in an effort to imitate the* FATHER*'s alb. He kneels.)* Go ahead.

(FATHER *places rosary.)*

GUSTAVITO: Thank you. Has anyone else ever worn this rosary besides you?

FATHER: Not since my parents gave it to me. No.

GUSTAVITO: So it's just you and me. Who do you confess to?

FATHER: I go to another church. A priest in another parish.

GUSTAVITO: I thought for a second you were gonna tell me you don't sin. Do priests have a club?

FATHER: No. Maybe you should give me back my rosary now.

GUSTAVITO: Still, if you walk down the street you can always spot each other. That's kinda neat, isn't it? *(He studies the rosary.)* It's beautiful.

FATHER: You're a good boy, Gustavito.

GUSTAVITO: Everybody says so. Can I say one prayer with it on?

FATHER: All right.

(GUSTAVITO *prays silently. He crosses himself and removes the rosary.)*

GUSTAVITO: Mercy makes promises. She makes a bargain with God and if she gets what she wants she'll do a novena or a week of rosaries. Does that work?

FATHER: Sometimes God listens. Sometimes He'll take pity.

GUSTAVITO: Can I put the rosary back on you?

(FATHER *bends over slightly.* GUSTAVITO, *who is kneeling, cannot reach him.)*

GUSTAVITO: You have to kneel.

FATHER: No, you stand.

GUSTAVITO: This is a holy ritual. You gotta kneel for these things.

(FATHER *kneels.* GUSTAVITO *is placing the rosary around the* FATHER*'s neck, who places his hands on* GUSTAVITO*'s hands to guide them.)*

GUSTAVITO: Maybe I can confess you. I can be a priest trainee.

(FATHER *stands.)*

GUSTAVITO: But you probably don't have that many sins. Not like me. And I don't even remember sinning that much.

FATHER: Gustavito, when you come to visit me, let's just keep it a secret, okay? Just between us two.

GUSTAVITO: Like best friends?

FATHER: Like best friends.

*(*JUNIOR *is smoking on the fire escape.* GUSTAVITO *enters the fire escape carrying two glasses of Tang. In the living room we can see the sewing dummy with a semi-fabulous wedding dress on it. Every time we see the wedding dress it has become more and more elaborate.* NORRY *and* MERCY *fuss around the dummy.* NORRY *has brought a large sequined spider that he moves from place to place on the dress. After every new placement he will take a few steps back and turn away from the dress only to spin around again quickly to get the full "surprise" effect of the newest location.)*

JUNIOR: Took you long enough.

GUSTAVITO: You wanted me to add sugar, right?

JUNIOR: Don't give me lip 'cause I'll throw you the fuck offa here.

*(*GUSTAVITO *sits, sipping his drink.)*

GUSTAVITO: I hope it don't rain.

JUNIOR: If it does we just wait right here. I ain't going in there while the freak is there. It's not even supposed to be here while we're here. *(He looks down.)* Oh shit man, there's Zoraya. Hey, Zoraya. *(He makes kissing noises.)* Hey, baby, don't be acting so fucking stuck up. It's too late for that. I had you.

GUSTAVITO: She don't like you.

*(*JUNIOR *hits him, hard.)*

JUNIOR: If you cry and get Mercy out here I'll crack your head.

*(*GUSTAVITO *cries quietly.)*

(Inside)

NORRY: I've tried to convince myself, but honey this spider ain't working.

MERCY: Who ever heard of a spider on a wedding dress?

NORRY: This dress is never gonna be finished.

MERCY: Forever in the making.

NORRY: It has to be special.

MERCY: Trust me, on you it'll be special.

NORRY: Did you wear white?

MERCY: Fresh.

NORRY: So sensitive.

MERCY: I can still wear white. I'm kidding.

NORRY: I don't think you are.

MERCY: And you're right. It's none of your business.

NORRY: Doctor Norry is in. How to get a man? Honey hush, you've come to the right place. 'Cause there's a right way and a wrong way and the wrong way just sends them running. Trust me, I know.

MERCY: Hand me the scissors.

(NORRY does. MERCY very carefully snips away stray threads as NORRY speaks.)

NORRY: How to keep a man? Ooooh, you've got to keep him interested.

(GUSTAVITO leans in to listen.)

NORRY: Find out what his fantasies are. Find the ones he doesn't even know about himself. If you can do that, you'll own him. Lust has a very short leash. How to get rid of a man? Kill him.

(MERCY laughs.)

MERCY: Ave Maria, Norry.

NORRY: No, I'm serious. Men don't understand from goodbye unless they're the ones saying it.

(Fire escape)

GUSTAVITO: What's a fantasy?

(JUNIOR takes out another cigarette.)

JUNIOR: It's what I am to Zoraya. She just be dreaming about me day and night. *(He bangs on the window.)* Hey, let's wrap it up in there.

GUSTAVITO: Junior, teach me how to smoke.

(JUNIOR hands him the lit cigarette from his own mouth.)

JUNIOR: Knock yourself out. *(He lights another one for himself.)* No, breathe in through your mouth and out through your nose. Like this. *(He demonstrates.)*

GUSTAVITO: Did Kiko teach you how to smoke?

JUNIOR: Man, Kiko wouldn't know how to shit if Mercy didn't tell him how. He is totally pussy whipped by her. I don't have any respect for him. Love fucks you up. It's true.

GUSTAVITO: Zoraya went in her house.

JUNIOR: I ain't blind. I saw it.

MERCY: Once a year I get violets. A little bouquet in the fall. I never know who sends them. "Secret Admirer".

NORRY: Yeah?

MERCY: For a week after I get them Kiko is very nice to me.

NORRY: I'm surprised he doesn't throw them out.

MERCY: He wouldn't dare. I'd kill him. They're mine. The only thing in this house that's mine. Third wife.

NORRY: What happened to the other two?

MERCY: Consuelo died and Esperanza just up and disappeared. I still think she's gonna walk in someday and take back everything.

NORRY: He'd be a fool to give up somebody as special as you. I gotta go. Don Kiko should be home soon. *(He collects his things.)*

MERCY: See you tomorrow?

NORRY: Like always. You want to come to the club sometime?

MERCY: You always ask.

NORRY: Well, you always tell me no.

MERCY: I can't.

NORRY: Someday we'll do a number together, okay?

(They kiss each other on the cheek. NORRY *exits.* MERCY *goes to the window.)*

MERCY: You can come in now.

JUNIOR: Not until you fumigate.

*(*GUSTAVITO *enters living room.)*

GUSTAVITO: Be nice to Junior, he got love trouble.

*(*JUNIOR *enters and smacks* GUSTAVITO, *who in turn hits him back.)*

GUSTAVITO: I didn't say nothing.

JUNIOR: It's that nothing that's gonna get you killed.

*(*MERCY *hits* JUNIOR *while trying to keep* GUSTAVITO *and* JUNIOR *apart.)*

GUSTAVITO: Like it's my fault Zoraya thinks you're stupid.

(In this exchange of smacks, KIKO *enters. He is drunk and embraces* MERCY *from behind and tries to kiss her.)*

MERCY: Get the hell off me.

KIKO: Come on, Mercedita, just one little kiss.

*(*MERCY *pushes him off.)*

MERCY: Oh, fuck, now I gotta get my hammer.

(She exits into the kitchen. KIKO *follows her. Their arguing voices are heard by* JUNIOR *and* GUSTAVITO. GUSTAVITO *puts his hands on his ears and tries to sing loudly to drown out the argument.* JUNIOR *takes his pack of cigarettes and throws it to* GUSTAVITO. JUNIOR *motions him to be quiet.)*

JUNIOR: Sssh. Just don't set this dump on fire.

(The arguing slowly fades as JUNIOR *exits.* GUSTAVITO *puts a cigarette to his lips and strikes a match. Lights fade except on match.* GUSTAVITO *lights his cigarette. Lights come up on* GUSTAVITO *smoking in the rectory. Enter* FATHER.*)*

FATHER: Put out that cigarette.

GUSTAVITO: No.

*(*FATHER *takes the cigarette out of* GUSTAVITO*'s mouth.* GUSTAVITO *flinches.)*

FATHER: You can't go home smelling of cigarettes.

*(*FATHER *begins smoking the cigarette.)*

GUSTAVITO: Hey, that's mine.

FATHER: That's mine, what?

GUSTAVITO: That's mine, Father.

*(*FATHER *sits, and continues to smoke cigarette.)*

FATHER: Is it yours?

*(*GUSTAVITO *nods.)*

FATHER: If it's yours, come get it.

*(*GUSTAVITO *slowly approaches* FATHER.*)*

FATHER: I shouldn't be smoking it if it's yours. It is yours, isn't it?

*(*GUSTAVITO *nods; he is now standing next to* FATHER.*)*

FATHER: Take it from me.

*(*GUSTAVITO *reaches for the cigarette.)*

FATHER: Slowly.

*(*GUSTAVITO *moves slowly.)*

FATHER: You know, we can both smoke it. We can share.

*(*GUSTAVITO *hesitates.)*

FATHER: There won't be much cigarette left. Take it from my mouth.

*(*GUSTAVITO *moves to do so.)*

FATHER: Gently.

(GUSTAVITO does. FATHER exhales.)

FATHER: Now put it in yours.

(GUSTAVITO does.)

FATHER: Smoke.

(GUSTAVITO does.)

FATHER: Inhale deeply.

(GUSTAVITO does and coughs.)

FATHER: Put it back in my mouth.

(GUSTAVITO does.)

FATHER: Hold it close to me. So that my lips can reach out and touch it. Where did you get the cigarettes? Your hand is shaking. Stop it. Bring it closer to my lips.

(GUSTAVITO does.)

FATHER: You stole them, didn't you?

GUSTAVITO: Yes, Father.

FATHER: Put it in my mouth.

(He inhales deeply.)

FATHER: Cigarettes are bad for you.

GUSTAVITO: Yes, father.

FATHER: And so is stealing. Hold it away from me. Did you steal anything else while you were waiting for me?

GUSTAVITO: No, father. I would never do that.

FATHER: How do I know? Smoke, please.

(GUSTAVITO puts it to FATHER's lips.)

FATHER: How do I know what a common thief would do? Hold it away from me.

GUSTAVITO: I'm going to burn myself, Father.

FATHER: Yes, you just might. Keep holding it.

(The cigarette is dangerously near the end. GUSTAVITO winces in pain.)

FATHER: If you drop it I will burn for your sins.

(GUSTAVITO begins to shake.)

FATHER: You lie, you steal. Why are you so bad?

(GUSTAVITO is crying now.)

GUSTAVITO: I don't know, Father.

FATHER: Put the cigarette down.

(GUSTAVITO does. FATHER blows on GUSTAVITO's fingers.)

FATHER: They're not burnt at all.

(GUSTAVITO begins to blow on the FATHER's fingers.)

FATHER: Why don't you go home? Please. I am not the proper friend for you. If you come back I'll have to go. Please don't do this to me.

(GUSTAVITO exits. A subway car. NORRY is standing; enter GUSTAVITO.)

TOUGH: *(V/O)* Any faggots on this train? I want all faggots off this train.

(NORRY grabs GUSTAVITO by the back of the neck and kisses him full on the mouth.)

NORRY: What was that? You wanted to help all faggots get off on this train? Don't worry about me, hon, I'm doing okay on my own. But, any straight boys who have never lusted after other boys on this train? That's a much more interesting question. Let's see a show of hands. And don't lie. I know who you are. Just look me in the eye and say it. This is our stop.

(NORRY taps GUSTAVITO on the shoulder.)

GUSTAVITO: I...

NORRY: You want to stay on this train by yourself?

(NORRY gets off the subway. GUSTAVITO hurriedly follows him.)

GUSTAVITO: You could have gotten us killed.

NORRY: They'd have to stop blushing first. Pendejo boys. No cojones kids on that train, honey. All they can do is beat you up.

GUSTAVITO: Kill you.

NORRY: Okay, so kill you, big deal. I was in high heels and I was chased by a bunch of these guys. They caught me and beat the shit out of me. I didn't hang up my heels. I just made them higher. I am a kamikaze queer. My first boyfriend was an inflatable doll. I think his name was Scott. You're a little far from home. This is my neck of the woods. Give you a tour?

GUSTAVITO: Of what?

NORRY: Paradise. How old are you again?

GUSTAVITO: Thirteen.

NORRY: So which is it? Twelve or God forbid, eleven? *(Silence)* Don't tell me ten. It's a good thing I woke up feeling motherly. I'll show you around, but be careful. The streets are hungry for cute boys.

GUSTAVITO: I'm not cute.

NORRY: No, you're not. But with my help you could be. I'm bringing you into a bar.

GUSTAVITO: They won't let me in.

NORRY: Oh, so you've tried already. I don't think you're ready yet, but just so you can see that you're not missing a whole lot. Knew you were gay the second I laid eyes on you.

GUSTAVITO: Huh?

NORRY: Now when we enter, own it. Let all the eyes hit you at once.

GUSTAVITO: They'll knock me off my feet.

NORRY: How can they, baby, if you don't give a shit? *(Before they enter* NORRY *stifles a theatrical yawn.)* Lead with the attitude.

(He walks in, followed by GUSTAVITO.*)*

NORRY: Let them take you in. Chill, bitch. This race is in slow mo.

*(*GUSTAVITO *nervously looks around.)*

NORRY: You better look cool or you'll answer to me. Raise your eyes slowly. Make eye contact. Lock into position. Now break. Break! You have to do it before they do. You have to win. Close your mouth, dear. We're window dressing, not window shopping.

GUSTAVITO: I can't breathe.

NORRY: Breathing's overrated. But if you must breathe do it so it makes you look like the hottest person in the world. Touch the back of your neck.

GUSTAVITO: What?

NORRY: Right hand, slowly on the nape.

*(*GUSTAVITO *does.)*

NORRY: Now turn, just the head.

GUSTAVITO: Left? Right?

NORRY: Left. Make that eye contact.

*(*GUSTAVITO *does.)*

GUSTAVITO: Who? Oh.

NORRY: One down. Sixty-nine to go.

(GUSTAVITO *bites his lower lip.)*

NORRY: Oooh. Self taught?

GUSTAVITO: What?

NORRY: And coy.

GUSTAVITO: That guy smirked at me.

NORRY: Sure, 'cause he can't have you. The bottom line is you never lose. Gustavito, never let yourself lose. Do you wanna dance?

GUSTAVITO: I'm not ready. Don't do this to me.

NORRY: What am I doing? *(Playfully)* What am I doing?

GUSTAVITO: I don't know how to do this.

NORRY: Ah, so pure. So innocent. Let me explain it to you so you can understand it. *(Screams)* You like dick!

(GUSTAVITO *disappears into his hands.* NORRY *points at him and speaks to the crowd.)*

NORRY: Right here, right now, my buddy boy here likes men. He likes all men. Sweaty men, clean men, dirty men. Tall, good-looking men and the men that might not grab your attention at first sight but know enough to call a trick by their rightful name. Old men, young men. No, I don't think younger would be physically possible. But he's flexible. He's poised and he can be yours for the low low price of a drink and a smile. He'd prefer someone nice but is willing to negotiate. *(Returns his attention to* GUSTAVITO*)* That was cruel, wasn't it?

GUSTAVITO: Yes.

NORRY: It's a gift.

(GUSTAVITO *begins to cry on the bar.)*

NORRY: Hey, hey. I'm sorry. Wait a second. It's a man, isn't it?

(GUSTAVITO *nods.)*

NORRY: The man has not been born who is worth one of your tears.

(GUSTAVITO *cries louder.)*

NORRY: Louder doesn't mean you love him any more. Now shut up.

(GUSTAVITO *does.)*

GUSTAVITO: I want money for the jukebox.

NORRY: So you can put on some sorry-ass "my man just left me" song? I don't think so.

GUSTAVITO: He doesn't love me.

NORRY: My God, a drama queen at your age.

GUSTAVITO: He doesn't.

NORRY: Do you even know what love is?

*(*GUSTAVITO *gives him a dirty look.)*

NORRY: Hey, for heartbreak to exist the heart has got to be in some real danger. Imaginary lover, imaginary heartbreak. It's a rule. Don't go breaking rules on me, honey.

(The living room. MERCY *has fallen asleep attaching seed pearls to* NORRY's *wedding dress. She has aimed a desk lamp to the folds of the skirt and pulled up a chair upon which she now sleeps. The only light in the room is from the desk lamp.* KIKO *enters. He turns on the light and turns it off quickly after seeing that* MERCY *is asleep. He gently walks up to her, but does not touch her.)*

KIKO: You're gonna go blind. *(She does not stir. He looks at the wedding dress in admiration.)* You have an art, my Mercedes. *(He studies her.)* It should have been you. First and for always.

(He tries to pick her up; she whispers in her sleep.)

MERCY: Norry.

*(*KIKO *rises and exits.)*

(Later, GUSTAVITO *is waiting for* JUNIOR *on the front steps.)*

GUSTAVITO: Hey, Junior.

JUNIOR: Hey, stupid. *(He is about to enter their building.)*

GUSTAVITO: Don't go up there. Zoraya's up there. She's talking to Kiko.

JUNIOR: About what?

GUSTAVITO: About you and shit and how you won't leave her alone.

JUNIOR: That's bullshit.

GUSTAVITO: She's got Kiko all worked up. She said she don't want nothing to do with you.

JUNIOR: Oh yeah? Let her tell me to my face. *(He again is about to enter the building.)*

GUSTAVITO: Kiko's gonna make you apologize to her.

*(*JUNIOR *stops.)*

GUSTAVITO: He's got his belt around his shoulders and after you apologize he's gonna beat you right in front of her. Zoraya said she don't like you and she never gave you—

JUNIOR: She's lying.

GUSTAVITO: —any indication that she was—

JUNIOR: That is such fucking bullshit.

GUSTAVITO: —interested or nothing. Her father's upstairs, too.

(JUNIOR is defeated.)

JUNIOR: She's gonna have my baby.

GUSTAVITO: When?

JUNIOR: Someday.

GUSTAVITO: Did she ever like you?

JUNIOR: She was fucking crazy about me. In school, she was like the one who would follow me in the hallways. See? This is woman, Gustavito. My mother dies, your mother leaves, and Mercy's like counting the goddamn days until she's outta here. Women leave. That's it. You treat them right, you treat them wrong, they leave.

GUSTAVITO: Mercy's not going no place.

JUNIOR: You wait and see.

(GUSTAVITO digs into his pocket and gives JUNIOR some money.)

GUSTAVITO: I took this from Kiko's wallet. Go to the Fairmont and see a double feature. Zoraya will be gone by then.

(JUNIOR takes the money.)

JUNIOR: I love her, you know? You tell me what I'm doing wrong, 'cause I don't see it. She's supposed to be mine.

GUSTAVITO: Junior, maybe I'm in love, too.

JUNIOR: You better not be. *(He exits.)*

GUSTAVITO: Please don't ruin it for me.

(It begins to rain. The FATHER's living quarters. GUSTAVITO enters; he is obviously quite drunk.)

GUSTAVITO: Father?

(FATHER enters. They stare at each other.)

GUSTAVITO: Hi.

FATHER: Go home.

GUSTAVITO: *(Laughs)* I'm all wet.

FATHER: Don't you have an umbrella?

GUSTAVITO: I lost it. I didn't want to tell Kiko. Umbrellas cost money, you know.

(FATHER exits offstage.)

FATHER: Wait right there. Don't move around a lot. Take off your shoes.

GUSTAVITO: I was walking, that's where I was. I stole a bottle of Don Q from Kiko so I'm a little bit a lot of lit. But that's okay cause that the only way sometimes you can talk, right? The rain tastes pretty good. If you lean back you can get it in your mouth. Just keep your eyes closed.

(FATHER enters with towel.)

FATHER: You didn't take off your shoes.

GUSTAVITO: You told me not to move.

FATHER: Take off your jacket and your shoes.

(GUSTAVITO removes his jacket.)

FATHER: Give it to me.

(FATHER takes the jacket and spreads it out on the altar railing. GUSTAVITO is having trouble untying his laces.)

GUSTAVITO: I can't get the knot untied. They're wet.

FATHER: Hold on. *(He gets on his hands and knees and tries to untie the laces.)* Why do you knot them?

GUSTAVITO: I'm sorry. *(He looks down at the FATHER and laughs.)* I do this for Kiko.

FATHER: Is he your father?

GUSTAVITO: Yeah.

FATHER: Then call him your father.

GUSTAVITO: Then what do I call you?

(FATHER removes one sneaker.)

FATHER: You can untie the other one.

(GUSTAVITO sits on the floor and removes his other sneaker. FATHER crouches behind him and dries his hair. GUSTAVITO begins to pray.)

GUSTAVITO: Every time I make a mistake I have to start again. Sometimes a whole day goes by and I can only say one prayer right. I start thinking about other things. *(He looks away from the FATHER.)* I love you.

FATHER: Don't say that.

GUSTAVITO: I walked around a lot all night trying to talk myself out of it, but it's not happening. No no no no no. *(Holds on to the chair. Steadies himself.)* To your face. Drunk? I'm not that drunk. I will remember this. You hear me?

FATHER: Yeah.

GUSTAVITO: 'Cause you're all quiet, so...make me nervous. Do we kiss now?

FATHER: No.

*(*GUSTAVITO *slides down the chair. He is now kneeling.)*

FATHER: You have to go home.

GUSTAVITO: Hey hey.

*(*FATHER *goes to* GUSTAVITO *and tries to help him stand.* GUSTAVITO *tries to kiss him.* FATHER *turns his head.)*

FATHER: Come on, sit down.

GUSTAVITO: You sit and I'll sit on your lap.

*(*FATHER *lowers* GUSTAVITO *onto the chair. He kisses* GUSTAVITO*'s hair.)*

GUSTAVITO: We'll go someplace where I'm not stupid and you're not a priest.

(A knock is heard.)

FATHER: Get back in the chair.

GUSTAVITO: That's my brother and I'm a gonna kick his ass. That's—

FATHER: Be quiet.

GUSTAVITO: —who it is, you know.

FATHER: Sssh.

GUSTAVITO: I'm afraid—

(More knocks on door)

JUNIOR: *(Voice only)* I can get real loud out here.

GUSTAVITO: —if I close my eyes I'm gonna drown.

*(*GUSTAVITO *leans against* FATHER *and collapses.* FATHER *carries him to the bed and lays him down.)*

JUNIOR: *(Voice only)* Don't try to hide behind stained glass.

*(*FATHER *opens the door.)*

FATHER: Is there something I can do for you?

JUNIOR: Fuck you. I just want my brother.

FATHER: He's not here.

JUNIOR: I have a hard time believing that. Maybe I should just call the cops so they can look.

FATHER: There's a pay phone on the corner. *(Pause)*

JUNIOR: He comes by you send him home.

FATHER: Why?

*(*JUNIOR *punches* FATHER *in the stomach, who crouches in pain.)*

JUNIOR: My hand slipped. Stupid questions do that to me.

*(*FATHER *is about to step outside but he hears* GUSTAVITO *moving on the bed.* GUSTAVITO *has gone under the covers and removed his shirt. He throws it at* FATHER*'s feet.* JUNIOR *does not see it, and* FATHER *slowly inches it away by using his foot.)*

FATHER: If you don't leave right now I'll be the one calling the police.

JUNIOR: Home. The second you see him.

*(*JUNIOR *exits.* FATHER *turns to see* GUSTAVITO *sleeping on his bed.* FATHER *holds the tee shirt in front of himself and looks in the mirror. He sees his reflection and also sees* GUSTAVITO *sleeping. He goes to the bed and stands by it.* GUSTAVITO *takes his hand.)*

GUSTAVITO: Thank you. If I couldn't see you anymore I would kill myself.

FATHER: No, you wouldn't.

GUSTAVITO: I love you more than anybody else.

FATHER: Go to sleep.

GUSTAVITO: My head is spinning.

FATHER: You'll be fine.

GUSTAVITO: Tell me you love me. And tell me we can be together.

FATHER: No, we can't.

*(*GUSTAVITO *struggles to sit up. He puts his arms around* FATHER*'s neck and closes his eyes.)*

GUSTAVITO: I'm safe. I'm not going.

*(*FATHER*'s arms slowly embrace* GUSTAVITO.*)*

GUSTAVITO: I love coming to church to hear you talk to God. Sometimes I imagine it's just you, me, and God. And He listens to you, you know, 'cause you like know all this stuff. And I feel stupid proud just watching you....I would kill myself.

*(*GUSTAVITO *tries to kiss* FATHER *on the lips;* FATHER *moves away.)*

FATHER: When you imagine that it's just you, me, and God, does God ever say anything?

*(*GUSTAVITO *has fallen asleep.)*

FATHER: I need to know if He talks to you, because He doesn't talk to me.

*(*FATHER *puts* GUSTAVITO *back on the bed. He exits to the church area and kneels before the cross.)*

FATHER: I'm going to lose this war.

(The living room. NORRY *is wearing a showgirl outfit and standing by the wedding dress. He sings simply and sweetly.)*

NORRY: *(Sings)* I've locked my heart
I'll keep my feelings there
Said I've stocked my heart
With icy frigid air
And I mean to care for no one
Because I'm through with love

I'm through with love
Won't ever fall again
Said adieu to love
Don't ever call again
For I must have you or no one
And so I'm through with love

*(*MERCY *applauds while* JUNIOR *joins in, sarcastically.)*

JUNIOR: Adios, loca.

*(*NORRY *grabs his crotch in a response.* JUNIOR *calls out the window.)*

JUNIOR: Gustavito!

MERCY: He's in church.

JUNIOR: No, he's not.

MERCY: Yes, he is.

JUNIOR: It's eight at night.

MERCY: So? The priest will bring him home.

JUNIOR: ...Yeah, okay. *(He exits.)*

NORRY: You know, every time I see one of those *Bride* magazines I get all confused. White? Off white? Cream? Chartreuse?

*(*MERCY *studies* NORRY.*)*

MERCY: No matter what I would do to myself I could never look as beautiful as you do now.

NORRY: Mercedes.

MERCY: The miracle maker. La milagrosa.

(NORRY stands behind the dummy. It's almost as if he's wearing the wedding dress.)

NORRY: What do you think?

(MERCY smooths out the skirt.)

MERCY: I'm afraid of the day it'll be finished.

NORRY: I can chart our history on this dress. When we had fights, when we made up. When we did each other's hair.

(MERCY begins to adjust the bodice.)

(GUSTAVITO rises and enters the church area, where he kneels, lights a candle, and begins to pray. Behind the church where FATHER has parked his car, JUNIOR enters with a tire iron.)

JUNIOR: You know, Padre, I warned you about leaving your car just anywhere. Nothing is safe anymore.

(JUNIOR brings the tire iron crashing down on the FATHER's car. GUSTAVITO is lighting another votive candle. The lit candles surrounding him illustrate how long he has been at it. JUNIOR continues trashing FATHER's car. Image wise, it's almost as if JUNIOR's rage is making him pure. The sound of the car being destroyed is slowly replaced by a hymn. The sound increases as the demolition of the car increases.)

(GUSTAVITO continues his ritual—each candle, each prayer more impassioned than the last.)

(JUNIOR is circling the car, searching for something else to destroy. He kicks in the front passenger window and tries to do the same with the rear window. Glass enters his shoe. He screams, but cannot be heard above the hymn. The volume begins to decrease. JUNIOR limps and exits.)

(MERCY touches the dummy's breasts. NORRY and MERCY are both frozen, staring at each other.)

NORRY: I don't trust straight people. *(He runs to the door.)*

MERCY: That door only works one way. You can't come back in.

(NORRY turns from the door. He takes off an earring and throws it at MERCY. She doesn't respond. He takes off his other one and throws it at her. She catches it and puts it on her ear.)

(KIKO is on the street. He has bought a bouquet of violets. He exits.)

(The church candle lights come up as the FATHER*'s car fades.* GUSTAVITO *is kneeling in prayer. Enter* FATHER*, carrying* GUSTAVITO*'s tee shirt. He stands, watching* GUSTAVITO*, and begins to pray.)*

GUSTAVITO: Excuse me, I was praying here.

FATHER: What are you praying for?

GUSTAVITO: I don't know.

FATHER: How can God grant your request if He doesn't know what it is?

GUSTAVITO: He knows. It's just me that don't know.

FATHER: That's a lot of candles. You must want something very badly.

GUSTAVITO: *(Correcting him)* Very much. I want something very much.

FATHER: But you don't know what it is.

GUSTAVITO: I'm not allowed to know....Father?

FATHER: Yes?

GUSTAVITO: Nothing. I want to wake up tomorrow and be you. That's what I want.

FATHER: I'm a thirty-year-old man, Gustavito, you're a ten-year-old boy. What you want is impossible. I'm not going to betray my life for you.

(He is about to exit, but stops to watch GUSTAVITO*, who continues to pray.)*

GUSTAVITO: God?

MERCY: *(To* NORRY*) Doesn't passion go where you live, either?*

*(*NORRY *approaches* MERCY*. He unbuttons her house dress; she unzips his dress and slides it down to his waist.* NORRY *stares at* MERCY*.)*

NORRY: No matter what I would do to myself I could never look as beautiful as you do now. *(He holds up his hand but cannot bring himself to touch* MERCY*.* MERCY *takes his hand and kisses it.)*

MERCY: Tell me I'm the first.

*(*NORRY *nods.* MERCY *gently puts his hand on her breast.)*

*(*JUNIOR *bursts in on* NORRY *and* MERCY*. His foot is bleeding and he leaves a trail of blood wherever he walks.* NORRY *and* MERCY *separate, but remain in partial undress.* JUNIOR *reels back as if struck.)*

JUNIOR: I'm not here. I'm not seeing this. Go someplace, Junior. Go someplace else.

*(*MERCY *and* NORRY *quickly put their clothes back on.)*

MERCY: Junior, wait a second.

JUNIOR: I'm not here. I'm not here. *(Slaps himself)* I'm not here. I'm not here. *(He points to* MERCY.*)*

JUNIOR: You. *(He begins to cry.)* Man, you like my mother. *(He begins to hit his head.)* But it's okay. It's okay. You can get the fuck out, too.

MERCY: Your foot. *(She tries to help him; he pushes her against the dummy.)*

JUNIOR: No, I'm okay. And when Kiko gets back, he'll take care of you. See, 'cause I was in church. I know what the priest is up to and I found Kiko so now he knows, too.

MERCY: Norry, get out of here.

JUNIOR: Oh, the freak's got plenty of time. First Kiko's gotta kill the priest and then he can come back and kill the both of you.

NORRY: And Gustavito?

*(*MERCY *runs out of the apartment.* NORRY *tries to follow but* JUNIOR *blocks the door.)*

JUNIOR: You wait here for Kiko, mother fucker.

*(*JUNIOR *punches* NORRY. NORRY *stomps on his bleeding foot.* JUNIOR *screams and falls on the floor. He writhes in pain.)*

JUNIOR: Everybody's gonna die. He's gonna kill everybody.

*(*NORRY *crouches next to him.)*

NORRY: I'm sorry.

JUNIOR: Now, you're scared, huh, mother fucker.

*(*NORRY *sits on the floor by* JUNIOR *and takes his foot in his lap.)*

JUNIOR: What you doing?

NORRY: Just gotta take off this shoe.

JUNIOR: Man, when Kiko come back he's gonna kill you. I'm a tell him everything.

NORRY: Honey, you don't know everything.

(He takes off JUNIOR*'s shoe.)*

JUNIOR: I think I'm gonna bleed to death.

*(*NORRY *shudders at seeing the bleeding foot. He very gently takes off the sock.)*

NORRY: No, you won't.

JUNIOR: You're gonna get blood all over you.

NORRY: I've had blood on me before. Been there. Done that. Packed a lunch. *(He reaches over to the sewing kit. He pulls out some tweezers.)*

JUNIOR: Whatta you gonna do?

NORRY: Pull out these glass splinters, stupid.

JUNIOR: If Kiko don't kill you, I will. I can't look.

NORRY: Look at the wall and tell me how you're gonna kill me.

*(*JUNIOR *looks away.* NORRY *starts to pull the glass splinters from his foot.* JUNIOR *grimaces in pain. He involuntarily grabs* NORRY*'s shoulder.* NORRY *rips pieces off the wedding dress and sops up the blood. He does not look up from his task.)*

NORRY: You're so much easier to be nice to when I don't have to look at you.

(Church. MERCY*'s voice calling out to* KIKO *is heard as if from very far away.* GUSTAVITO *rises. When he turns he sees the* FATHER.*)*

MERCY: *(Voice only)* Kiko! Kiko!

FATHER: Does He talk to you, because He doesn't talk to me.

GUSTAVITO: Nothing happens that God doesn't know about.
(He gently touches the FATHER*'s face. Very slowly, they kiss.)*

KIKO: *(Voice only)* Gustavito!

END OF ACT ONE

ACT TWO

(At Rise. The white, glowing cross appears. The Delgado family appears from behind it. They each carry a suitcase. They place their suit cases down and tilt the cross to the right. Airplane noise is heard. The cross has become an airplane. They make a small circle with it before returning it to its starting place.)

VOICE: Good morning. Now arriving at Gate 24 is American Airlines Flight 989 from New York. Welcome to Puerto Rico.

GUSTAVITO: Kiko told me he would kill the Father if I didn't come to Puerto Rico.

MERCY: Kiko told me he would kill Gustavito if I didn't come to Puerto Rico.

JUNIOR: Kiko told he would kill me if I didn't come to Puerto Rico.

KIKO: Their lips were touching. I don't know a lot but I know right from wrong. I know a sin when I see it.

(Lights up on the confessional. NORRY *enters the penitent's side. Silence.)*

NORRY: Is it my line?

FATHER: Forgive me Father for I have sinned.

NORRY: Okay. Forgive me Father for I have sinned.

FATHER: How long has it been since your last confession?

(Silence. NORRY *earnestly tries to calculate the time.)*

FATHER: Why are you here?

NORRY: When you took the vow, you knew you were giving up a whole lot, right? But you did it 'cause you had to. 'Cause the call was so strong you had to. It was like destiny, you know what I'm saying?

FATHER: In the least.

NORRY: No? I thought if anybody would know about denial it would be you. I confess, Father. *(Pause)* You are my last recourse. Trust me, the words Catholic and comfort don't go hand in hand in my brain. Okay, my sin. For the last three years I have dreamt of this woman. Going against everything I am. Everything I am happy to be.

FATHER: The problem is she's...?

NORRY: The problem is she's a she. The problem is I'm going to have to change who I am to love this person. The problem is we're not even the same size. I used to dream of being accepted, so I found a world, a small world, where I could be. Where if I follow the rules I could be accepted. But, I never stopped resenting the rights other people took for granted. The gentle kiss, the hand holding in public, the "Hello, we're a couple, we fuck, and how are you?" that men and women take for granted. Bitter? I left bitter in the dust. I see families, "traditional families", and I get teary-eyed even as I laugh at them. Aren't they just the stupidest thing? Hello? Are you still there? Hello?

FATHER: I'm here.

NORRY: Feel free to interrupt me at any time with those pearls of wisdom that are just dying to leave your lips.

FATHER: Let's leave my lips out of this.

NORRY: Done. I am happy to be who I am. I am proud to be who I am. So why can't I forget her? *(Pause)* Father, I think you know what I'm talking about. Can you broker a deal with God for me?

FATHER: I don't do that.

NORRY: If your God, *the* God, any God can take her away from my heart after these three years I will give them my plumage. Just give me peace...and give her happiness. That's it. That's my prayer.

*(*FATHER *leaves the confessional. Pause.* NORRY *approaches him. He takes off his wig and drops to one knee, takes the* FATHER*'s hand, and kisses it.)*

NORRY: This. Will take. Some getting used to.

*(*NORRY *exits.* FATHER *looks at his kissed hand. He crosses himself with it.)*

FATHER: Three years. Amateur.

*(*NORRY *and* MERCY *from Puerto Rico and New York)*

MERCY & NORRY: I don't even know where to look. She's forgotten all about me by now.

MERCY: I mean he. He's forgotten all about me.

NORRY: Packed up and left in the night.

MERCY: I dream of you.

NORRY: Bon voyage.

MERCY: Kiko would have killed you.

NORRY: Forget me.

MERCY: You're a tattoo on my memory.

NORRY: Stop that.

MERCY: You're the sheet I cover myself with at night.

NORRY: Would I still be beautiful to you now?

(FATHER and KIKO, from Puerto Rico and New York)

FATHER & KIKO: I am not a bad man.

KIKO: My family is sacred to me. As his God should be to him. I have a right to defend what's mine. I will not let my son drown.

(MERCY kneels. She is clothed in a white "habit" dress and wears a green belt made of yarn. She looks very plain except for the earring that she wears, the earring that NORRY threw at her.)

MERCY: Dear God, let's make a deal.

FATHER: Gustavito, your father loves you very much.

KIKO: Someday Gustavito will put his arm around me and thank me. Someday he will say, "Thank you, Kiko, for saving me."

FATHER: What did one father say to the other father?

KIKO: I would make an empty space where that kiss had lived. You have to understand—

FATHER & KIKO: I am not a bad man.

FATHER: What did one father say to the other father?

KIKO: My son is telling me he loves him.

FATHER: What did one father say to the other father? Why did you take my son from me?

KIKO: Why did you take my son?

(GUSTAVITO and JUNIOR in Puerto Rico. GUSTAVITO lights up a cigarette.)

GUSTAVITO: I don't know when I'm going but I'm going.

JUNIOR: It's your fault we're here.

(Pause. They stare at each other.)

JUNIOR: Accept it, deal with it, grow from it.

(They share the cigarette back and forth. They smoke in silence.)

JUNIOR: Of all the people in the world to be nice to me why did it have to be him? He tore a piece off that wedding dress that mattered so much to him, for me. He did that for me.

(GUSTAVITO puts his head in his hands.)

JUNIOR: Gustavito.

GUSTAVITO: Sssh. I'm trying to send a message.

(After a few beats JUNIOR *assumes* GUSTAVITO*'s position and also tries to send a message.)*

FATHER: I think about him sometimes.

KIKO: He'll thank me someday.

FATHER: Sometimes.

*(*MERCY *crosses herself and rises.)*

MERCY: Don't forget about me, God.

GUSTAVITO: *(To God)* Please let me be angry. It's the only way I'll survive.

NORRY: My idea of an anatomically correct woman was always Barbie. Talk about your midlife crisis slash career change.

*(*KIKO *has his pants rolled up. He is in the "river" where he first saw* MERCY*, who enters carrying a mug of coffee and a towel.)*

MERCY: Hey, Mister, this is the Gomez River. You're on our property.

*(*KIKO *and* MERCY *laugh.)*

KIKO: And then did I fall or did you push me in?

MERCY: You fell, but I helped you out.

KIKO: Yeah, you took my hand. And then Consuelo came running up to me with a towel. Esperanza was (looking on.)

MERCY: *(Cutting him off)* Esperanza wasn't even home that day. I brought you some coffee. *(She hands it to him. He tries to take her hand; she slips it away.)*

KIKO: It's not the same island we left.

MERCY: Kiko, maybe we should go back. The boys aren't happy and you can get your old job back.

KIKO: No.

MERCY: Gustavito's eyes have died.

KIKO: Tell me, do you think my family respects me or fears me? *(Silence)* If anybody tries to leave I will kill them. You have my permission to tell them. I'm an ugly man.

MERCY: My mother used to say, "The uglier the man is the better."

KIKO: No, Mercy. I'm an ugly man. *(He blows on his coffee.)* If I throw this in your face, I would disfigure you. You would be ugly, too. You would never leave me.

MERCY: Drink your coffee.

KIKO: The water is nice and cool. You want to join me?

MERCY: I have no intention of joining you. Get out of there. You're gonna get sick and I'm not in the mood to take care of you.

(KIKO gets out of the water. MERCY goes to dry his feet but he stops her.)

KIKO: No, let Gustavito do it. *(He calls out.)* Gustavito! Gustavito! Gustavito! I guess Gustavito can't hear me.

MERCY: That must be it.

(KIKO takes the towel. He sits on the ground and dries his feet. He laughs at himself.)

KIKO: I can't sleep. I was ready to kill the Father but I would've had to have killed Gustavito, too. He wouldn't let me hurt his priest, his Father. I make the Father kneel. I make him beg my forgiveness and then I start beating him. You try to pull me off, but nothing can stop me. And then Gustavito's hands are hitting me. He loves this man who is weeping on the floor. And I grabbed Gustavito's lips. I was going to rip them off, because I couldn't stand looking at them anymore, and there was no fear in him. None. There's fear, shame in the Father but none in the boy. So, why can't I sleep? I keep seeing Gustavito without a mouth. *(He runs his fingers gently over MERCY's mouth.)* A gaping hole where that kissed had lived. Poof. No more kiss.

(FATHER has finished Mass. He takes GUSTAVITO's baseball cap from its hiding place and places it on the altar and talks to it.)

FATHER: Not a great Mass today. Attendance is down, apathy is up. I think pizza for dinner would be good tonight. What do you think? Maybe. You'll get married someday to a very nice woman. Someone who will love you very very much. And you'll have lots of children. I think you will make a wonderful father. And someday, way down the line, you'll come back with your family and walk into my church and you'll be happier than I ever could have made you. Maybe you'll even forget all about me. God bless you. For the first time in my life I'm afraid of dying. Of taking all my secrets with me. With all that would be unsaid and a God who never knew me. You were supposed to show me the way. I can fake this. I have for years.

(GUSTAVITO kneels. He takes the FATHER's rosary from his pocket and places it around his neck.)

GUSTAVITO: Por mi culpa, por mi culpa, por mi gran culpa. I want to make You a promise, God, but I don't know what You want.

(JUNIOR enters the river site.)

KIKO: You want to go in? The waters feel good.

JUNIOR: Nah.

KIKO: You know, let's get a couple of beers. Huh? Okay? Okay. Maybe we can go play some dominoes. I always said you were too young, but you're a man now. You understand. You're not a boy anymore, you know I did the right thing.

JUNIOR: ...Yeah.

KIKO: Mercy don't get it. You see the promise dress she's wearing? She's made a promise to God. And Saint Judas. That's what the green belt is for. Saint Judas, the patron saint of impossible causes.

JUNIOR: She's just got a guilty conscience, that's all.

KIKO: She's made a promise with Saint Judas that I die soon.

*(*FATHER, *in the confessional, lights a cigarette, smokes for a few seconds, then holds it away from himself as* GUSTAVITO *did.)*

NORRY: *(Sings)* Jesus loves me this I know
For the Bible tells me so
Little ones to Him belong
They are weak but He is strong
(He stands behind the wedding dress.)
Well, technically, I'm not wearing it. Right, God? Uh, God?

*(*JUNIOR *enters* MERCY *and* KIKO*'s bedroom. From a trunk he removes a glittery dress that* MERCY *had started, but never finished, for* NORRY. *He stares at it.)*

JUNIOR: Fucking freak.

(He moves the dress as if it were worn by someone. He sings, very softly.)

JUNIOR: I'm through with love
I'll never fall again
Said I'm through with love
(He is stumped momentarily for the words.)
La la la la la la
For I must have you or no one
And so I'm through with love

*(*MERCY *enters.)*

MERCY: We're gonna eat.

JUNIOR: Yeah, okay. *(He remains frozen in place.)*

MERCY: Now.

*(*JUNIOR *throws the dress on the floor.)*

MERCY: Go get your brother.

*(*JUNIOR *exits.* KIKO *enters.)*

MERCY: We're going to eat.

KIKO: Uh-huh. What's with you?

MERCY: Nothing.

KIKO: You want a kiss?

MERCY: No.

KIKO: Are you sure?

MERCY: I'm very sure.

(MERCY has turned away.)

KIKO: ...Do you want me dead? I'm not stupid, you know.

MERCY: I know. You're the king of this house.

(JUNIOR enters.)

KIKO: Where's Gustavito?

JUNIOR: He's not hungry.

KIKO: Go get him.

JUNIOR: He's praying.

KIKO: In this house we eat when I say we eat. Serve the food. He's gonna eat. 'Cause I want him to eat.

MERCY: Please don't do this, Kiko.

KIKO: 'Cause I said he was going to eat.

(Lights down on family. Up on FATHER.)

FATHER: I was giving Mass the other day and my mind went blank. Just before we got to the Communion. Blank. I throw in a little Latin, bless the crowd a couple of times. No one noticed. And I thought to myself, "It finally happened. God is gone." I'm giving Communion and looking at the little wafers and I want to laugh, "This is supposed to feed your soul? You couldn't even make a good sandwich out of this." I'm the only one who sees this. They all believe. They all believe me as I bless them in the name of the Father, the Son, and the Holy Gustavito, amen. One after another they don't hear it. At my next Mass I will recite the twenty-third psalm, the psalm of Gustavito. They will not hear that, either. No, they won't.

(Lights up on the Delgado family at the dinner table. KIKO walks GUSTAVITO to the table. GUSTAVITO is dressed older; his walk and manner are more in keeping with the teenage boy he is. KIKO places a plate of food in front of GUSTAVITO, who does not eat. KIKO becomes enraged and forces a handful of food into GUSTAVITO's mouth. KIKO and JUNIOR exit. MERCY tries to clean up a bit and then exits. She reenters with a bag of Oreos, and sits next to GUSTAVITO and begins to eat.)

MERCY: Don't even ask for one 'cause they're all mine. And they're so good. Look, Gustavito, Oreos.

(GUSTAVITO continues to stare blankly ahead.)

MERCY: You remember staying home when you were sick and I would give you Oreos for breakfast? I loved when you stayed home with me. All you had to do was sneeze and I would keep you out of school. You were such good company and you would help me sew. Well, look at this, I never noticed before but they look like chocolate Communion wafers, don't they? *(Silence)* Well, yes, Mercy, I guess they do. Fat Communion wafers for fat Catholics. I can let you have one, but that's all. Just one. *(She eats another Oreo. She takes the top off one and with great care she begins to apply the white cream filling as eye shadow to herself.)* When men leave us all we have left is our looks.

(GUSTAVITO embraces her.)

MERCY: Sssh, Gustavito. Mercy, mercy me.

GUSTAVITO: Help me, I miss him so much.

MERCY: I don't want to hear this.

(GUSTAVITO stares at her.)

MERCY: Yes I do.

GUSTAVITO: I know I'm not wrong.

MERCY: Gustavito.

GUSTAVITO: I'm going back someday.

(She gives him an Oreo.)

MERCY: Uh-huh.

GUSTAVITO: I don't know when I'm going—

MERCY: —but I'm going.

GUSTAVITO: Do you think God forgot about me?

MERCY: No.

GUSTAVITO: I made a promise with Him. It was my first one so I thought He would listen. You still think he will, right?

MERCY: Yeah, of course. I made a promise too. *(She points to her outfit.)* I want Esperanza to come back for Kiko.

(KIKO sits by the river, reading a telegram.)

MERCY: And she'll be just as she was when she left him. Like I saw them leave. Kiko came looking for me to say goodbye, but I hid. I could see the rice pelt them and I saw as he took her arm. He picked up Junior and hugged Esperanza. Then he kissed her like I've never seen anybody kiss anybody. And they got into a car and drove off. To the airport. New York. The next time I saw him he came to get me. But he wasn't smiling like that day with her so I didn't think I should smile either.

GUSTAVITO: Do you love him?

MERCY: I love him with pity. That's no way to love someone.

GUSTAVITO: And if he were to change.

MERCY: I'm never going to get the same smile I saw that day. Not from him.

*(*KIKO *enters; he kisses* GUSTAVITO*'s head.)*

KIKO: Get your things together. We have to go back. Esperanza is dead. Her other family wants her buried in New York.

*(*MERCY *exits.* GUSTAVITO *rises and as he heads to the church,* KIKO *exits while speaking.)*

KIKO: We will only be going back for her wake and the funeral. Four days. That's it. You hear me? You hear me, Gustavito.

*(*GUSTAVITO *enters the church.)*

FATHER: We're not opened right now.

GUSTAVITO: Hey Father. Back from the dead, so to speak.

FATHER: Gustavito.

GUSTAVITO: Have I changed a lot? What do you think, Father?

FATHER: When did you get back?

GUSTAVITO: I came back for my mother's funeral. Not Mercy, Esperanza. My real mother. I haven't seen her yet. They could put any corpse in front of me and I would be expected to cry on cue.

FATHER: Whatever happened, Gustavito, she was your mother.

GUSTAVITO: Yes, Father, she was. Hey, it was an excuse to come back. I'm all cured now.

FATHER: I didn't know you were sick.

GUSTAVITO: You were the cause. First love, worst love.

FATHER: Gustavito.

GUSTAVITO: Gustavo.

FATHER: Gustavo. You're a young man now.

GUSTAVITO: Fifteen. You wanna sit?

FATHER: How's your family?

GUSTAVITO: Everybody's fine. Real happy, like always.

FATHER: Good. Does God still talk to you?

GUSTAVITO: I talk to Him.

FATHER: Does he listen?

GUSTAVITO: I'm here, aren't I? So who replaced me? Who became your altar boy?

FATHER: Domingo.

*(*GUSTAVITO *laughs.)*

GUSTAVITO: I knew it. Little prick. Excuse me. Before I left I was going to kill him. Seriously. Well, as seriously as a ten-year-old can think of something like that.

FATHER: As I recall you were a very serious ten-year-old.

GUSTAVITO: I didn't think you had any memory of me. So, first I was going to kill him then I decided it should be you. And me. I can't believe I'm confessing out here. Can we go to the confessional?

FATHER: This is fine.

GUSTAVITO: Please.

*(*FATHER *enters his space in the confessional and* GUSTAVITO *enters his.)*

GUSTAVITO: Forgive me Father for I have sinned. It has been five years since my last confession.

FATHER: Go ahead.

GUSTAVITO: You used to say, "Go ahead, my son."

FATHER: Go ahead, my son.

GUSTAVITO: So, you glad to see me? *(Silence)* Okay, where did I leave off? Oh yeah, I was going to kill us. I started hating you and me and I figured the pain would be better than the hate. But I didn't, so. Does that count as a sin? I thought it, but I didn't do it.

FATHER: Do you repent?

GUSTAVITO: I can't. Anyway, I don't have to. I'm over it. You.

FATHER: That's good.

GUSTAVITO: It's different for you. You never had anything to get over, right?

FATHER: You know, I could never find my rosary after you left.

GUSTAVITO: That's a shame. This little box was the safest place in the world to me. Where I first heard your voice, you remember?

FATHER: I really should get back.

GUSTAVITO: To what? I am over you.

(FATHER tries to leave the confessional; GUSTAVITO quickly follows him and grabs his wrist.)

GUSTAVITO: I am over you.

FATHER: I'm not going to fight with you, Gustavito. I did the right thing.

(GUSTAVITO slowly lets go of FATHER's wrist.)

GUSTAVITO: Did God tell you that? 'Cause he didn't tell me. Gotta go. Oh, my penance.

FATHER: Please don't come here again.

GUSTAVITO: That ought to do it. *(He reaches into his pocket and pulls out the FATHER's rosary.)* I was saving it for you. Here. *(FATHER does not move. GUSTAVITO dangles the rosary.)* Take it.

(FATHER does.)

GUSTAVITO: I wasn't going to keep it from you. It's yours. What's the Latin word for impossible? Never mind. I'm over you.

(GUSTAVITO exits. FATHER kneels, holding the rosary.)

FATHER: I've missed you.

(The funeral home. The Delgado family, all in black, sit watching the casket. KIKO wipes away a tear. He is the only one to do so.)

MERCY: *(To casket)* You still beat me, didn't you?

GUSTAVITO: *(To casket)* Wow, my lips. You have my lips. I've never seen them on anybody else. Well, I'm sorry you're dead. I mean I would be sorry if anybody was dead. I don't know you, Lady, but I'm sure you had your reasons for going. I hope I wasn't one of them. You didn't leave me any hints. You didn't leave me anything. Except your lips. Listen, if I lean over the coffin it's so they'll think I'm crying 'cause I guess I should. But I can't. Sorry.

(He leans over the casket. At first he is just awkwardly over it, then he slowly embraces it. He rises and runs off. JUNIOR follows him.)

KIKO: I am less angry than I thought I would be. I swore the next time I saw you I would kill you. Once again you got the better of me. So, I will never know why you walked out. Why you cheated on me. They don't know about that. I told everybody you just left. Were you happy after you left? I know you never were with me. I've tried harder with Mercy but you know

I'm not a man of a lot of words. Junior's fine. He remembered you for a while. He thinks women always leave. For him they have. Gustavito. Gustavito is broken. And I don't know how to fix him. Sitting next to him and I don't know him anymore. Esperanza, if you can help at all with this. Don't forget me, Esperanza. And forgive me for whatever I did. *(He sits back down and tries to take* MERCY*'s hand.)*

MERCY: What's the point? ...I want a little happiness, Kiko.

(Under MERCY*'s speech* KIKO *will softly repeat the words "Caress me.")*

MERCY: A little for me, you know? I don't want to resent you anymore, Kiko. Your touch never belonged to me. You gave it to Consuelo, then Esperanza, how could I expect you to have any left over for me? I would like to see the boys every so often, if that's okay. And maybe someday we can see each other without you hating me.

(She rises. KIKO *grabs her hand and kisses it. She exits.)*

KIKO: Mercedes.

*(*GUSTAVITO *enters the gay bar where* NORRY *once took him. The music that played there instantly plays again as he opens the door.)*

GUSTAVITO: Have you seen Norry? Have you seen Norry? Have you seen Norry? Have you seen Norry? Norry, where are you? I need you.

*(*FATHER *enters the penitent's side of a confessional. His side is lit while the other side remains dark.)*

FATHER: Forgive me Father for I have sinned. It has been an eternity since my last confession. I'm sorry, a week. God has placed a test in my path. Again. If I could understand His motives in doing this I might be better equipped to fight against it. He has placed me in the path of myself. I worry I will not have the strength to deny myself as I should. As He wills it. I need to be blind. I need to be immune.

GUSTAVITO: Cruise me, mother fucker. *(Dismissively)* Hi. *(Pause)* Pisces. *(Pause)* Oh, and you? *(Pause)* Neat. No. *(Pause)* No. *(Pause)* No. Yeah, you can buy me a beer. I'm old enough. How old are you? *(Pause)* I figured. No, I said "It's sunny out today." *(Pause)* Okay, so it's sunny out tonight. *(Pause)* My name is...Junior. *(Pause)* Uh, thank you, but I don't dance.... I have a heart condition. Nice meeting you, too.

FATHER: Any chance of me getting a sign from God? I don't mean to be disrespectful. I just feel I've been abandoned by Him. You're in that little black box because you want to be, right? That must make all the difference in the world.

*(*GUSTAVITO *touches the back of his neck, and he bites his lower lip; in short, he does everything he learned from* NORRY*, all to no avail. He comes across more as desperate than sexy. He spots someone.)*

GUSTAVITO: Hi. *(His eyes follow the person as he leaves.)* Bye. *(He smells under his arm pits.)*

FATHER: Would God be terribly upset if I were happy? No, you ask Him. I don't think He wants to speak to me.

(The Delgado family living room in New York. Everything is as we last saw it. The wedding dress is still on the dummy. There are old blood stains on parts of it and the pieces that were ripped off have not been replaced. JUNIOR*, using his key, enters. He looks around a bit before* NORRY *enters.)*

JUNIOR: You didn't change the locks.

NORRY: Did Mercy come back with you?

JUNIOR: They told me you took over our apartment.

NORRY: I pay the rent. It's mine now.

JUNIOR: Hey, I don't care. *(He walks up to the wedding dress.)* You kept my blood. That's sweet.

NORRY: So, is Mercy back?

JUNIOR: You look different.

NORRY: I'm going for a new look. Norry Lite.

JUNIOR: Look, I came here to say I was sorry for the way I treated you.

NORRY: And just how did you treat me?

JUNIOR: Like shit.

NORRY: Today my son you are a man.

JUNIOR: You did okay by me. I mean, I don't know why, but.... How did you get Mercy to fall in love with you?

NORRY: You think she's in love with me?

JUNIOR: If...if you wanted to make somebody fall in love with you, what would you do?

NORRY: I don't know how to do that.

JUNIOR: Yes, you do.

NORRY: Junior, I'm flattered. But one of us would have to be sedated. Just buy me a little love trinket and we'll call it even.

JUNIOR: Not you, you freak.

NORRY: Hey!

JUNIOR: I'm sorry....I'm sorry. There's...somebody I love, but I don't think they love me. I figured if you made Mercy fall in love with you, you could do anything.

NORRY: Are you sure it's not me? I've had straight boys fall in love with me before. I'm probably the first queer you ever talked to without using your fists.

JUNIOR: I'm not in love with you. You looked better in a dress.

NORRY: Maybe you would, too.

*(*JUNIOR *turns to leave.* NORRY *stops him.)*

NORRY: Okay, okay, okay. Do something romantic for them. Serenade...her. Nobody does that anymore.

JUNIOR: Like in the middle of the street? No, I don't think so.

NORRY: She'll love it.

JUNIOR: Gimme something else.

NORRY: No. You want love to be easy? Well, it's not. Go out there and make a fool of yourself like the rest of us. Take the leap or get the hell out of the way and let the rest of us commit suicide.

JUNIOR: What if I die?

NORRY: You die. And guess what? It doesn't get any easier the next time.

JUNIOR: Mercy will be at the Rosado Funeral Home on Tremont. Six p m. We're even now, okay? *(He exits.)*

NORRY: If you say so.

*(*NORRY *and* MERCY *meet again; she is dressed like a man. She in a black version of her "promise" outfit. He sees her walking by and stops her.)*

NORRY: Mercedes.

MERCY: Norry? *(She circles him.)*

NORRY: I'm sort of trying to be Norberto now. Simple, tasteful. Plain.

MERCY: Plain?

NORRY: Plain me. And you? *(He circles her.)*

MERCY: I made a promise.

NORRY: To what? Disappear?

MERCY: It doesn't matter anymore.

NORRY: Love your earring.

MERCY: A peacock gave it to me.

(NORRY produces a small bouquet of violets from his jacket.)

NORRY: Here. These are for you. I know you like them.

MERCY: I like them because someone gave them to me. It wasn't you.

NORRY: No. No, it wasn't.

MERCY: Junior tells me you took over our apartment?

NORRY: Yes, I did. It's just the way you left it.

MERCY: Tell me, is the wedding dress still there?

NORRY: Of course.

MERCY: And it's still not finished?

NORRY: It'll never be finished. I tried to finish it but I don't know how to sew, Mercedes. Do you hear what I'm telling you? I don't know how to sew. And at this late stage in my life I don't know if I could even learn to thread the needle.

MERCY: It's okay.

NORRY: I want to make you happy and if my sewing would do that I would try with all my might, but needle and thread are not what I'm about. That's why I searched you out a million years ago.

(Silence)

MERCY: Two virgins.

NORRY: Two virgins.

MERCY: Do you want to learn?

NORRY: To sew?

MERCY: To sew.

NORRY: I... *(She kisses him.)*

MERCY: Your hands are still softer than mine.

NORRY: You didn't expect me to throw out thirty-eight years of skin care products, did you?

(Pause. MERCY puts NORRY's earring on him.)

MERCY: This belongs to you. I borrowed it and you must always return what you borrow. And I *want* you to have it back. It looks good on you.

NORRY: I can't change who I am, Mercy, and I don't want to, but I want to love you.

MERCY: ...Can I stay with you for a while?

NORRY: Until we finish the wedding dress.

(They shake hands.)

MERCY & NORRY: Deal.

*(*JUNIOR *enters. He whistles a verse of* "I'm Through with Love" *as* MERCY *and* NORRY *exit. He carries a brown paper bag with a bottle in it. He takes a long drink and sits on the stoop and begins to cry.)*

JUNIOR: I'm fucked.

*(*GUSTAVITO *enters church and spots* FATHER.*)*

GUSTAVITO: Hi, Father. I'm going back to P R today. *(He holds up his hands in a truce sign.)* I just came to say 'bye.

FATHER: 'Bye.

(Silence. GUSTAVITO *initiates an awkward handshake.)*

FATHER: I'll pray for you.

GUSTAVITO: Yeah, I'll pray for you, too. Betcha I pray longer than you do.

FATHER: No fair, He listens to you.

GUSTAVITO: He used to.

FATHER: He will again.

(Silence. GUSTAVITO *turns to leave.)*

GUSTAVITO: If He does maybe He can tell me why you laid there on the floor and let Kiko beat you? Why you begged for forgiveness as if we had done something wrong?

FATHER: Because we did.

GUSTAVITO: What I felt...feel for you is not wrong and what you feel for me is not wrong.

FATHER: I don't have any right to feel anything for you. Where are we supposed to go? What are we supposed to do? Gustavito, I know the world that we live in, there is no place for us there.

GUSTAVITO: Am I the only one in love here? *(Silence)* Just tell me, am I the only one in love?

FATHER: Before I met you, I can honestly say I have never loved anything. Or anyone. Not the way you do. I envy people who say they would die without something. To die of desire. You were away from me for five years and it didn't change your obsession.

GUSTAVITO: I'm not obsessed.

FATHER: What would you call it?

GUSTAVITO: I'm in love.

FATHER: Gustavito, I would give half of my life if things were different, but they're not.

GUSTAVITO: Then will you wait for me if I wait for you? *(Silence)* At ten years old I was ready to do battle with Kiko for you. I was willing to take on my whole entire world for you, but I can't do this by myself anymore. I can't. I can't. *(Turns to leave)* I won't. *(He exits.)*

FATHER: God?

*(*GUSTAVITO *enters* NORRY*'s apartment.)*

NORRY: Life would be so much simpler if one could fall in love with the "right" person.

GUSTAVITO: Tell me about it.

NORRY: I'm a good man, an honorable man, but am I her man?

GUSTAVITO: Do you love her?

NORRY: ...Yeah. My dear, how did this happen?

GUSTAVITO: You know, sometimes when things really got bad for me I would try to imagine what you would do and it would make me smile.

NORRY: You were laughing at me?

GUSTAVITO: Never. I gotta go back.

NORRY: You can stay with Mercy and me.

GUSTAVITO: I don't want to risk running into him. You know he really does love me in his own way.

NORRY: Uh-huh, that was tired even before it got out your mouth.

GUSTAVITO: I would do anything if he would take me back.

NORRY: Back where? You haven't been anyplace.

GUSTAVITO: Why do goodbyes have to hurt so much?

NORRY: Goodbyes are a piece of cake. It's the hellos that leave the scars. *(He holds him gently and kisses him on the forehead.)* Nobody falls in love faster than a virgin. And that includes forever-young drag queens.

(From outside they hear singing.)

JUNIOR: *(Voice only)*
I'm through with love
I'll never fall again
Said I'm through with love
La la la la la la

For I must have you or no one
And so I'm through with love

*(*NORRY *looks up. He goes to the fire escape.)*

GUSTAVITO: What's that?

NORRY: The most romantic thing that never happened to me.

GUSTAVITO: Is it for you?

NORRY: It's on loan.

*(*GUSTAVITO *exits.* NORRY *climbs out on the fire escape.)*

JUNIOR: I'm through with love
I'll never fall again
Said I'm through with love
La la la la la la
For I must have you or no one
And so I'm through with—

(He and NORRY *face each other.* JUNIOR *runs off.)*

NORRY: All I did was be nice to him, and now I've gone and confused him.

(On the street)

GUSTAVITO: Hey.

JUNIOR: Just don't say nothing, okay? I'm gonna get married.

GUSTAVITO: To who?

JUNIOR: I said not to say nothing. *(He makes a fist as if to hit him.)* Zoraya the second. Actually her name is Nydia but she said it's okay for me to call her Zoraya.

GUSTAVITO: Do you love her?

*(*JUNIOR *casually punches* GUSTAVITO *in the jaw, hard.* GUSTAVITO *falls to the ground.* JUNIOR *continues, very matter of factly.)*

JUNIOR: She is marrying me to get out of her house. Her parents are too strict. She told me, so it's cool.

GUSTAVITO: Do you sing to her?

JUNIOR: I don't have to. *(He gets down on the same level as* GUSTAVITO.*)* This is strictly a no-risk, no-commitment situation. And when she leaves it won't hurt. At all. Thinking ahead. That's what you should be doing.

GUSTAVITO: So why were you singing to Norry?

*(*JUNIOR *locks him in a hammerlock, squeezing the air out of him.)*

JUNIOR: One thing you have to decide is what you're willing to give up. I know my limitations and I can sense you're getting dangerously close to yours.

(He releases GUSTAVITO, *who collapses, gasping for air.)*

JUNIOR: I'll get married. I'll have a kid. Fuck, I'll kill Norry if I have to but I'll be okay. This I swear to you.

GUSTAVITO: And Zoraya?

JUNIOR: Ah, she never did give me the time of day. God invented love to punish people. *(He suddenly stops. He "sees" Zoraya. He waves to her.)* Hey, Zoraya. *(Sings)* For I must have you or no one—

JUNIOR & NORRY: And so I'm through with love.

*(*JUNIOR *looks from Zoraya, to* NORRY*'s fire escape, and back to Zoraya again.)*

JUNIOR: Oh, fuck. Stereo.

*(*KIKO *goes to* NORRY, *who is still on the fire escape.)*

KIKO: How do I compete with you?

NORRY: You don't.

KIKO: *(Pulls out a small bouquet of violets)* What do I do with these?

NORRY: Tell her.

KIKO: Someone told me she already has herself another man. Delicate, gentle, some would even say beautiful.

NORRY: Some would. I'm not holding her here with any threats. She's here because she wants to be here.

*(*MERCY *takes the wedding dress off the dummy.)*

KIKO: You're not afraid of me.

NORRY: Let her see you with the violets in your hand. Let her know you were her secret admirer.

KIKO: I couldn't do that.

*(*MERCY *takes off her habit dress.)*

NORRY: Couldn't. What a big word.

*(*KIKO *brings the violets to his heart.* NORRY *goes inside.* JUNIOR *enters the street, carrying his bottle of malt liquor. He sits on the floor. From his pocket he takes out a deck of cards and begins to play solitaire, in the same manner that* KIKO *did.)*

JUNIOR: When did I become my father?

*(*MERCY *puts on the wedding dress. She reaches out for* NORRY.*)*

MERCY: It's still not finished. Come, my peacock.

(KIKO is standing outside the door of NORRY's apartment.)

(FATHER is performing a wedding ceremony. GUSTAVITO enters, standing in the back of the church.)

FATHER: ...here before your friends and family. Do you, do you Jorge take Carmen as your lawfully wedded wife from this day forward, to have and to hold in sickness and in health as long as you both shall live?

GUSTAVITO: *(Softly)* I do.

FATHER: And. And do you Carmen take Gustavito, I'm sorry, take Jorge as you lawfully wedded husband from this day forward, to have and to hold in sickness and in health as long as you both shall live? Can you do that, Carmen? *(Pause)* Yes. Of course you can. You love each other. Here, before God, I now declare you husband and wife. You may kiss the bride.

(GUSTAVITO takes a step forward and the FATHER takes one back.)

GUSTAVITO: I'm sorry I wasn't born earlier. I'm sorry I bother you. I'm sorry I cause you pain. Hey, Father, which is the bigger sin? Yours or mine?

(GUSTAVITO comes up behind KIKO.)

GUSTAVITO: Hey, we leaving or what?

(Lights down, then up on GUSTAVITO, who comes up behind KIKO at apartment door. KIKO nods. He begins to trace a heart on the door using the violets.)

GUSTAVITO: It's just you and me, huh, Kiko?

(KIKO places the violets on the floor outside the door. He puts his arm around GUSTAVITO. They both stare at each other. KIKO removes his arm. They both put their hands in their pockets.)

(MERCY looks at NORRY. She shakes her head, sits him down, and pulls out a make-up kit. She begins to apply make-up to his face. NORRY takes her hand, kisses it, and begins to apply make-up to her.)

(KIKO goes to where JUNIOR is playing cards and moves one of them for him.)

KIKO: A spade is a spade.

(JUNIOR collects his cards and turns away from KIKO.)

JUNIOR: It's called solitaire.

(GUSTAVITO and KIKO begin to walk. Enter FATHER.)

FATHER: Gustavito.

(GUSTAVITO and KIKO stop walking. KIKO continues.)

KIKO: Come on.

FATHER: Gustavito.

KIKO: Come on, we're gonna miss the plane.

(GUSTAVITO is standing between the two fathers. He looks at FATHER and shakes his head. He walks toward KIKO.)

FATHER: If you wait for me I'll wait for you.

(GUSTAVITO turns to FATHER.)

FATHER: If you wait for me I'll wait for you.

KIKO: If you go to him I'll kill him.

(GUSTAVITO takes KIKO's hands and places them on his throat.)

GUSTAVITO: Then you have to kill me. 'Cause I love him. To your face, Kiko, I love him.

(KIKO embraces GUSTAVITO.)

KIKO: If you come with me I'll close my eyes to everything. You will never tell and I'll never know.

GUSTAVITO: I want you to know, Kiko. I need you to know.

(KIKO kisses GUSTAVITO and exits.)

FATHER: I don't want to be afraid anymore.

(The stage darkens as the cross begins to glow.)

GUSTAVITO: And I don't want to have to apologize or deny or look down.

(FATHER nods and takes GUSTAVITO's hand. They kneel before the cross.)

FATHER: Father, I want you to meet Gustavito.

GUSTAVITO: He knows me.

FATHER: Father, I want you to meet me.

END OF PLAY

FLOORSHOW: DOÑA SOL AND HER TRAINED DOG

ORIGINAL PRODUCTION

FLOORSHOW: DOÑA SOL AND HER TRAINED DOG was first produced by Brooklyn Playworks on 22 October 1987. The cast and creative contributors were:

SOL .... Katherine Marie Loague
SON .... Michael Caron
WOMAN .... Stacie Linardos
GIRL .... Daphne Rubin-Vega
BOY .... Carlos Linares
CUSTOMER .... Wellington Santos
CUSTOMER/NURSE .... Christine Vanacore

Director .... Phylis Ward Fox
Choreograpy .... Michael Caron
Sets and costumes .... Neil Jacob
Lights .... Chris Kondek
Sound .... David Ravel
Stage manager .... Rona Bern

FLOORSHOW: DOÑA SOL AND HER TRAINED DOG was subsequently produced by Latino Chicago. The cast and creative contributors were:

SOL .... Laura Ceron
SON .... Edward Torres
WOMAN .... Michelle Banks
BOY .... Daniel Sanchez
GIRL .... Justina Machado
NUN .... Laurie Martinez
Various players .... Gregorio Gomez
.... Frank Rosario

Director .... Juan Ramirez
Costume design .... Michelle Banks
Light design .... Juan Ramirez / Frankie Davila
Sound design .... Juan Ramirez / Edward Torres
Assistant director .... Michael Torres

CHARACTERS

SOL
SON
WOMAN
GIRL, WOMAN *as a child*
BOY, SON *as a child*

Five people to play all other roles

(Lights rise. Low, sensual music is heard. The SON*'s chant begins in the background, rising and falling as in a wave.)*

SON: I didn't kill her, I didn't kill her, I didn't kill her, I didn't kill her, I didn't kill her, I didn't kill her, I didn't kill her, I didn't kill her, I didn't kill her, I didn't kill her.

WOMAN: Oh, yes you did.

SON: I didn't kill her.

WOMAN: If you didn't, who did?

SON: I didn't kill her.

WOMAN: But you had to.

SON: I didn't kill her.

WOMAN: We all saw it.

SON: I didn't kill her.

WOMAN: Prove it.

SON: I didn't kill her, I didn't kill her, I didn't kill her, I didn't kill her, I didn't kill her, I didn't kill her.

(Lights up slowly on a small, cheaply furnished room. There is a bed, a table with a loaf of bread and a knife, and off to the side a closet. Opposite the closet there is a vanity table with a mirror and a bench. Seated at the vanity is SOL, *a young woman who is busy making herself beautiful.)*

(Her two children are helping her get ready. The BOY *(11)* is very protective of his little sister *(*GIRL, *age 9)*, who is deaf, dumb, and blind. He puts the brush in her hand and guides it through their mother's hair.)

BOY: See how soft?

(A knock is heard. SOL *leads the* BOY, *who leads the* GIRL, *into the closet.* SOL *gives the* BOY *a loaf of bread and puts her children into the closet. The lights dim. In the silhouette we see* SOL *take off her robe and a* MAN *enter. He begins to kiss her. The lights fade on them and come up on the closet door. The* BOY *is shaking the closet door, begging to be let out.)*

BOY: Sol! Sol!

(The closet moves forward. The door bursts open and now the BOY *is a* MAN *in a straight jacket. He is alone. His sister is gone. Lights dim on him and come up on another part of the stage.* SOL *is crouched behind a door. Her hands are covered in blood. The lifeless body of her daughter lies next to her. An angry mob approaches her home.)*

#1: Murderer!

#2: Whore! Come out and pay for your sins.

*(*SOL *cowers behind the door.)*

#3: Only by purging her sin can we hope to cleanse this town.

#4: She has shamed us.

(The mob's fury is uncontainable.)

#1: Come out you whore! It doesn't matter where you hide. We will find you.

*(*SOL *looks at her daughter's inert body. She slowly stands and faces the door. Before she exits she absentmindedly wipes her daughter's blood off her hands and onto her chest. She opens the door. The crowd becomes silent and faces her.)*

SOL: Here I am. Well? You've been calling loud enough for me.

(#2 breaks from the crowd and slaps SOL. *Immediately, he drops to his knees.)*

#2: *(Screaming)* I can't see! I can't see! She's blinded me.

#1: She's a witch.

#3: Look at her. She's covered in blood.

#4: Her daughter's blood.

#2: Someone please help me. Please.

*(*SOL *approaches #2. The crowd fearfully backs away. She touches his eyes.)*

SOL: You can see.

*(*SOL *faints. #2 opens his eyes.)*

#2: I can see! I can see!

#1: She's a saint.

#5: She's cured him.

(The crowd gathers around SOL*'s prone body.)*

#4: Did you see how the blood on her chest glowed when she performed her miracle?

#3: She is one of God's chosen.

#1: Look at her. So beautiful.

#5: A goddess.

(#2 picks up SOL.*)*

#2: An altar. We must build an altar for our Doña Sol. Where she may preach to us and show us the way.

(The others begin building an altar for SOL.*)*

#5: She can perform miracles. She will set us free.

(The crowd begins to pray. We hear an occasional "Doña Sol" now and then. The GIRL *gets up; the dry blood is still on her chest. She looks out of* SOL*'s door and sees the crowd. She approaches them and points to her blood, but no one pays any attention. When the altar is finished, #2 places* SOL *on top of it.* SOL *regains consciousness and the crowd drops to its knees in prayer for her.* SOL *is like a cat, ready to flee, until she realizes the prayers are for her. She smiles and sits regally on her throne. The* GIRL *comes and lays at her feet. Lights out. Lights rise on* SON, *who is sitting on a bare floor in a straightjacket.)*

SON: Hypocrites.

*(*WOMAN *appears.)*

WOMAN: She really thought she killed me.

SON: I did, too.

WOMAN: And from my death a saint was born.

SON: Those people were so stupid. Willing to believe anything as long as it was impossible.

WOMAN: Why did she kill me?

SON: She could barely take care of herself, let alone two children.

WOMAN: But you took care of me.

SON: For always.

WOMAN: And you let her kill me.

SON: She looked me up; like now. Got me out of her way.

WOMAN: Why didn't she put us away together? Like she always did.

SON: Because you were broken. You were her broken doll. You couldn't see or hear or speak. You were so pretty, but you couldn't do anything. And I was born with a hole in my heart. A tiny little hole that prevented me from doing anything. So out of two broken children she made a whole one. She gave me your heart. My little sister's heart.

WOMAN: I'll always be better than you.

SON: I don't care.

WOMAN: Yes, you do. Even without a heart, without my sight... *(She covers his eyes.)* ...my voice... *(She covers his mouth.)* ...or my hearing... *(She covers his ears.)* ...I will always be better than you.

SON: I want to be good. Please help me. Don't make me jealous of you.

(The WOMAN *disappears as #1 enters as a* NUN.*)*

NUN: Your mother is here to see you. *(No response)* I said your mother is here to see you. You should be very proud. She's taken time out from her busy schedule to see you. You should be very proud. Anyone would want to trade places with you right now.

(The NUN *exits.* SOL *enters. She is wearing a house dress. Her hair is pulled back and she wears no make-up. She is smoking a cigar.)*

SOL: They tell me you're not eating. Hey this place is expensive, you might as well eat the food they give you. It's all paid for, Baby. You look better, you know. Soon you can come home. I'm dying to have you back with me, Baby. I miss you so much. The way only a mother can miss her son. Her only child.

(The SON *shifts away from* SOL.*)*

SOL: Everything's going so good for us. Why did you have to crack up like that, Baby? I love you, Baby. You're my best friend. You're the only man in my life, you know that, right? I want you to come home. And I want you to get well. *(She gently caresses his head.)* Will you do that for Mami? I'm such a big baby! I've had to sleep with the lights on since you've been gone.

SON: La bendición.

SOL: May God bless you and protect you.

*(*SOL *leaves. The lights follow her as she goes to her consultation area, which consists of a table and two chairs. Seated by the table with her back to the audience is the first in a series of customers.* SOL *sits facing the audience. She begins shuffling a deck of cards.)*

CUSTOMER: Oh please, Doña Sol, I need your help.

SOL: Everyone needs Doña Sol's help. Cut.

*(*CUSTOMER *cuts the deck.)*

CUSTOMER: It's my husband

SOL: I know what's wrong. Your husband has lost interest in you.
A woman has come between you.

CUSTOMER: Yes.

SOL: A beautiful woman. *(She puts the deck on the table.)* Cut into three piles.

*(*CUSTOMER *does.* SOL *takes the pile on the right and pushes the other two aside. She places the cards, face up, one by one in a circle formation.)*

SOL: He's seen other women before.

CUSTOMER: Yes.

SOL: But this one's different. She's carrying his child.

CUSTOMER: Please, no.

SOL: He wants to marry her. Has he asked you for a divorce?

CUSTOMER: No. I'm not even supposed to know about the other woman.

SOL: As if kissed lips could hold a secret. This woman called you.

CUSTOMER: Yes. She said she was going to take him away from me.

SOL: No great loss.

CUSTOMER: I have children, Doña Sol.

SOL: Ah yes, children. It's too late to correct that mistake. We'll have to take care of this woman, won't we? Her name is Leyda.

*(*CUSTOMER *nervously nods her head.)*

SOL: Write her name in your blood. Prick your finger and write her name on a piece of paper. Then put it in a glass full of water, make sure the glass is made of plastic, and put it in your freezer. Never take it out. Next, take a lock—

CUSTOMER: A lock?

SOL: Like any lock. Tie something of your husband's around it and throw it into the sea. Make sure you keep the key. He'll stay put with you where he belongs.

CUSTOMER: Oh, thank you. You don't know the relief I feel. How much do I owe you?

SOL: Whatever you feel is fair.

*(*CUSTOMER *pays* SOL *and kisses her hand.)*

SOL: Send the next one in.

*(*CUSTOMER *exits. Another enters and sits.* SOL *is already shuffling her cards.)*

SOL: Sit. You're having trouble...you're having trouble with your son. I may not be the best person to help you. My son is also very ill. We share that you and I. But yours, yours will recuperate. Mine. My baby. He lies. He's crazy. I think someone who was jealous of me put a curse on him. He makes up these incredible lies, and he knows they're lies. He knows they hurt me.

Why does he want to hurt me? I love him. *(She begins to weep.)* Go home. Tell them all to go home.

*(*CUSTOMER *exits as* SOL *weeps.* SON *is about to caress* SOL*'s head when she abruptly leaves. Enter* NUN*, who is busy studying* SON*'s chart. Off to the side, in a lower light, is a long narrow platform that is slightly higher than waist level. It is a diner.)*

NUN: You're cured now. *(She smiles and offers her hand. The* SON *clumsily takes her hand.)* You're a good boy.

(The NUN *exits. Lights dim on* SON *and rise on diner.* SON *enters, repeating softly to himself:)*

SON: I'm a good boy. I'm a good boy.

*(*SON *stands by someone and continues his soft chant. He/she gives him a dirty look and moves away. Someone else takes the place. Building his courage:)*

SON: I'm a good boy. I'm a good boy. I'm good.... It's a beautiful day today, isn't it. Not for everybody, of course, but me, I like a little rain. It looks like it's going to rain again, huh? Yeah. Do you want me to leave you alone? Can I buy you a cup of coffee? One coffee, please. If everyone would just discuss their differences over coffee there would be no more problems. It's the sensible thing to do. The adult thing.

(No one hears anything the SON *is saying.* #2 *turns his back on* SON*, who then goes to* #3.*)*

SON: I'm a good boy. One coffee for my friend, please. I'm not a boy. I'm a man; but if you asked me to prove it I couldn't. A nice boy. Never in the way. When Sol introduces me that way I feel I have to break something, throw a fit. Break the tension of being good. Everybody expects me to be good, but what if I'm not good enough?

(#4 *enters.* SON *runs to him/her.)*

SON: You think I'm a good boy, don't you? Coffee please. You've never seen me before, but I'm a good boy; wouldn't you say? Please, wouldn't you say? Have another cup, on me. I'm a good boy. Right? Who else buys you this much coffee? Tell me, who?! *(*SON *runs angrily to* #1.*)* It's Doña Sol, isn't it? So perfect. So beautiful. Cures your ills. Make you forget about me and all my coffee. All my sins. I love her, but she can't love a sinner. Say you forgive me. Sure, you drink my coffee but you won't absolve my sins. Say I'm a good boy, say I'm a good boy and I'll never love Doña Sol again.

(#5 enters.)

SON: Can I buy you some coffee, a sandwich, ice cream? What do you want? Just tell me what you want and I'll do it.

(Lights out. Lights up on DOÑA SOL*'s present-day bedroom. There must be a clear distinction between the bedroom of her past and of her present.* SOL *is dressed as before—simple housecoat, no make-up, and the ever-present cigar. The diner counter has become her bed and her vanity is off to the side.* SOL *runs up to* SON *and embraces him. For his part, he's not all too sure how he got there.)*

SOL: Oh, Baby, I've missed you so much. Give Sol a kiss.

SON: Uh, sure, Mami.

SOL: Ugh. Don't call me Mami. I'm young enough to be your sister.

SON: You look like shit, Sol.

SOL: It's too bad they didn't put a straightjacket on your mouth.

SON: It's true. You don't take care of yourself anymore.

SOL: Who have I got to look good for?

SON: Me.

SOL: *(Not hearing him)* When you're in my line of work you dress down.

(She begins to turn down the bed.)

SON: If you dress at all.

SOL: I was born into this, you know? Like you. What's the matter, too good to perform miracles?

SON: Not good enough.

SOL: Don't be silly, Baby.

(After SOL *is done with the bed, she places a sheet and pillow on the floor at the foot of the bed for the* SON*.)*

SON: I can't fake it like you can.

SOL: I don't fake shit.

SON: I can't be honest like you can.

SOL: You're okay.

SON: I'm ugly.

SOL: Of course you're ugly. You're my son.

SON: You're beautiful. The most beautiful woman in the world.

SOL: You're sweet, Baby. A fine son. You don't smoke or drink.

SON: I have a weak stomach. They make me nauseous.

SOL: You go to church every Sunday.

SON: I made a promise to go.

(SOL sits at her vanity and begins to put on cold cream and get ready for bed. WOMAN is on the other side of the vanity as SOL's mirror image, only she is doing the exact opposite of SOL—WOMAN is applying make-up and fixing her hair. SOL and SON don't hear each other.)

SOL: Everyone would always brag to me about how they'd see you going off to church on Sunday. How you always went to the very first Mass at six a m. And it wouldn't matter how late we'd been up the night before. I would hear you as you practically crawled out with the sun. Just so you could be the first one in church to greet God. That got me a lot of customers, Baby.

SON: I'd wake up at five-fifteen a.m. and go to the first Mass on Sunday. The first Mass was the shortest one. I could be in and out in half an hour. On my way to church once, a couple stopped me. I thought they needed directions so I stopped to help. The man grabbed my penis and laughed, "It's so small," and his woman laughed and called me ugly. I could never understand how God could let that happen to someone going to church. After that I always wore the tightest pants I had to church.

SOL: The priest would tease me and tell me he should give you your own set of keys to the church. He was crazy about me, Baby.

SON: I had to go to church because I had promised God that if the kids at school would stop making fun of me I would go to church.

SOL: Well, let's go to sleep, Baby. Tomorrow is a big day. Got to show you off to everyone. Let them see how I cured my baby. My ugly little baby.

(SOL and the WOMAN stand. SOL gets into bed and makes herself comfortable.)

SOL: I want to get an early start tomorrow . None of your dawdling in front of the bathroom mirror. Anyone would think you were a girl, staring at yourself in the bathroom mirror. You're not a girl, are you, Baby?

SON: *(Mesmerized by the WOMAN)* No, Sol.

SOL: Come give Sol a kiss.

(SON does not move.)

SOL: Baby.

SON: When the lights are out.

SOL: I don't look that bad, Baby.

(SOL lays back. WOMAN approaches SON. She lays on the bed with her feet by SOL's head and her own head inches from SON. She begins to fondle him. He loses himself in her. They kiss. Lights fade.)

SOL: *(Voice only)* How about my kiss, Baby?

(From the darkness SON *comes to the edge of the stage.)*

SON: She never asked me why I stare into the bathroom mirror. I knew she wouldn't. Some answers don't interest her. I don't see anything in the mirror. Not my reflection or my half-awake eyes that beg me to have mercy on them. I just don't see anything. But I'm not looking for anything either. I only know that when the water hits me I'll be officially awake; and I don't want to be. When my eyes are open everything gets taken away from me. You know, there's a moment when you're between being awake and being asleep, and your mind sort of freaks out because you can't move. Can't even open your eyes; like a coma. I always think I'm going to die if I don't wake up. I struggle so hard to move. And then I become exhausted and give up. That moment when I give up, when I recognize that the struggle is over and I've lost; that moment is delicious.

(Lights up on stage. On one side of the stage are SOL *and her worshippers. They are kneeling before her. She is shuffling cards and smoking a cigar. The worshippers are chanting her name and throwing out questions to her. Next to* DOÑA SOL *is the closet with its side facing the audience. The* SON *is inside, holding a box which he proceeds to open. The chant of "Doña Sol" is constant throughout this scene.)*

#1: I have lost my wife.

SOL: I will make her return to you.

(The SON *takes out an inflatable doll from the box. He begins to inflate it.)*

#2: I have lost my house.

SOL: I will get it back for you.

(The SON *is anxious about being caught. He blows up the doll hysterically.)*

#3: What will the number be tomorrow, Doña Sol?

SOL: Hey, show a little more respect.

#4: Don't ever leave us, Doña Sol.

SOL: Where would I go?

#5: I'm dying, Doña Sol.

SOL: You won't die.

#1: I can't breathe.

SOL: You can breathe.

#2: I can't cry.

SOL: And you can cry.

(The chanting builds in volume. The SON *is about finished inflating his doll. It now becomes clear that it is a female sex doll. The* SON *joins in the "Doña Sol" chant.* SOL *silences her worshippers.)*

SOL: My children, that's enough. Listen to me. I have a special surprise for you.

(The SON*'s chant continues nonstop, his volume rising as he caresses the doll.)*

SOL: You can hear him. Yes, my son has come home. I have cured him. He is here to take his rightful place next to me. Listen to him. There is true passion! There is true belief! Join him all of you.

(Her worshippers join in SON*'s feverish chant.)*

SOL: We must make him feel welcome. He has been away too long. My son. My son. My son.

(Lights on SOL *fade as the "Doña Sol" chant builds. As the* SON *reaches his climax he screams out his mother's name.)*

SON: Sol!

(The chant fades. Blackout. Lights up on closet. SOL *is inside holding a mostly deflated male doll.)*

SOL: There is nothing new under the sun, Baby. We've all seen it. Only I pretend to look the other way as I let my only child O D on desire. Let him feel guilty for what he feels. When he feels guilty he's indebted to me. Guilt is nine-tenths of the law. Nice boy. His father would say that he would beat manhood into him so my boy naturally assumes that being a man is painful. Then the man up and leaves without telling the little shit how to be a man. My son didn't know. He still doesn't know. Look at him. *(She holds up the doll.)* Is he half-empty or half-full? For an only child both of my children have given me nothing but heartache. And don't think I don't tell him, Baby.

(Under the last two lines the GIRL *appears on the other side of the closet. She repeats softly under* SOL*'s lines and twice on her own.)*

GIRL: If you believe I exist, I existed.

(Lights fade over closet and rise on SOL*'s consultation area.* SON *is sitting shuffling cards, smoking a cigar. A* CUSTOMER *sits, back to the audience, facing* SON.*)*

SON: Cut the cards into three equal piles starting from the left.

CUSTOMER: I want to find out who's put the evil eye on me.

(The SON *takes the pile on the left and pushes the other two aside.)*

SON: Did you bring a handkerchief?

CUSTOMER: Yes.

SON: It must be a silk handkerchief.

CUSTOMER: It is.

(The CUSTOMER *takes it out of his pocket.)*

SON: Tie it around your eyes.

(The CUSTOMER *does.)*

SON: Now I can see.

(SOL *enters.)*

SOL: You're padding your part, Baby.

SON: I was keeping your cards warm.

SOL: So now you're a card-warmer?

*(*SON *gets up.* SOL *sits with* SON *standing behind her.* SOL *notices a* CUSTOMER.*)*

SOL: What's this?

CUSTOMER: Someone has put the evil eye on me.

SOL: *(Sarcastic)* And you'd rather not see them.

CUSTOMER: Your son, Doña Sol—

SOL: Take it off.

SON: He'll see us.

SOL: That's silk, isn't it?

CUSTOMER: Yes, Doña Sol.

SOL: I love silk. May I?

*(*SOL *takes it from* CUSTOMER *and wraps it around her neck.* SON *will take an end in each hand and will begin to very slowly pull at them.)*

SOL: I see a lot of jealousy in your path. You're the kind of person who inspires jealousy.

CUSTOMER: That's true.

SOL: You're a hard worker. You mind your own business. Yet this person is jealous of you. Do you know where jealousy comes from?

SON: Fear.

SOL: This person is afraid of you. There's a part of you that reminds them too much of themselves. You frighten them.

CUSTOMER: I haven't done anything to anyone.

SOL: Sometimes that's enough reason. *(*SOL *looks up at* SON.*)* Tighter, Baby. I can still breathe.

(The SON *drops his hands to his sides.)*

CUSTOMER: What can I do?

SON: Move away.

SOL: And let the enemy win?

CUSTOMER: I will do whatever you say, Doña Sol.

SON: Put the evil eye right back on them.

SOL: Overzealous amateur.

SON: Then?

SOL: Isn't your father calling you?

SON: Or maybe it's my sister.

SOL: It can't be your sister. You killed her long ago.

CUSTOMER: I will do whatever you say, Doña Sol.

SOL: Whatever I say.

SON: He doesn't know any better.

SOL: But you do.

CUSTOMER: I will do whatever you say, Doña Sol.

SOL: Exactly as I say.

CUSTOMER: Whatever you say, Doña Sol.

SOL: *(Referring to* CUSTOMER.*)* He's a good son.

SON: *(Defensively)* Me, too. I am, too.

SOL: Did you finish your breakfast?

SON: Yes, Mom, and I walked the dog.

SOL: Good boy.

SON: I have to go to school now.

SOL: Did you wash behind your ears?

SON: Yes, Mommy.

SOL: You come straight home from school. You know how your father and I worry. There are a lot of crazies out there.

SON: I love you, Mommy.

SOL: I love you too, Beaver.

CUSTOMER: Doña Sol?

SOL: I know who is responsible for your evil eye. Go home, I'll take care of it.

CUSTOMER: Bless you, Doña Sol, and your fine son.

SOL: Don't encourage him.

CUSTOMER: How much do I owe you?

SOL & SON: Whatever you feel is right.

(The CUSTOMER *pays and exits.)*

SOL: I do a solo act, punk.

SON: I figured you might be lonely.

SOL: Maybe for a real man, but not for you, Baby.

SON: I'm not a real man.

SOL: No.

SON: But you still love me?

SOL: Yes.

SON: And my father?

SOL: He loved you most of all.

SON: And my sister?

SOL: You had no sister.

SON: I can't focus.

SOL: You were an only other child

SON: Yes, that's right.

SOL: My two and only.

SON: Why can't I keep that straight?

SOL: Your Sol loves you.

SON: Sol loves me?

SOL: Jump. Sit up. Roll over. Play dead.

*(*SON *does.)*

SOL: Good boy.

SON: I'm a good boy?

SOL: You're a good boy.

SON: The bestest? The bestest boy?

SOL: The bestest, Baby.

SON: Sol, I didn't mean to hurt her. I swear.

SOL: Be quiet, Baby. This is a Hallmark moment.

SON: Oh Sol, let's run away together.

SOL: And leave all this? This gravy train?

SON: Well, at least cut me in for some of the profit.

SOL: You don't need money, Baby. You don't need anything. You've got Sol. You're set for life.

WOMAN: *(Entering)* You always let her get to you.

SON: I do not.

SOL: I'm like winning the lottery.

SON: You couldn't talk, you couldn't see; she had to do something.

WOMAN: And you let her.

SOL: I think those doctors were right. That shock therapy has helped you.

WOMAN: What did you resent—that Sol loved me, too?

SON: She only loves me.

SOL: And I'm sure that in my own small way I helped.

WOMAN: Focus.

SON: I'm losing you.

SOL: A mother's love can work miracles.

WOMAN: But it can't bring back the dead.

SON: You were so beautiful.

WOMAN: Sol would walk with us. Her and her movie star looks and me a little replica of my mother. Being guided by my older brother...

SON: I don't remember that.

SOL: Only a mother can truly love you, Baby.

WOMAN: I was so pretty people would give me money. Just for being pretty. Did anyone ever give you any money for being pretty?

SON: I was a good boy.

WOMAN: Sol would look the other way.

SOL: The only one who will accept without question.

WOMAN: And you would help me put out my hand for the money. And I would curtsy, as you taught me. I was the one they liked.

SON: But not good enough.

WOMAN: Even broken I was better than you.

SOL: And forgive.

SON: So I took one of your dresses and put it on. It was very short and I looked very cute. Just like you. And I went out. No kid has self-respect when he's six years old; but my father did. They told him I was begging in the street in my sister's dress.

SOL: Only a mother.

SON: And he picked me up and carried me home. So gently. Even as people made fun of me and him. He proudly carried his son home.

WOMAN: He took off his belt and beat you in the street. He ripped my panties off your bottom and rubbed them in your face. "These are not yours," he screamed. He continued beating you until the game became too gruesome, even for the vultures.

SOL: A mother would do anything to protect her child, a true mother would, Baby.

SON: The next day he woke me up early and took me shopping. Anything I wanted he would get me. All I had to do was ask. Just me and him. He carried me home.

WOMAN: He rubbed my panties in your face.

SON: And when we got home he put me down and you were smiling. As if you could see me, as if you could hear what the people had said, as if you could say what they had said. You were smiling.

WOMAN: I was smiling.

(The BOY *walks across the stage carrying a knife.* SOL *follows him for a few steps, stops, and faces the audience.)*

SOL: I did what any mother would have done. Hell, the kid's gotta eat, right? And I gotta eat, too. Their father. I suffocated his father. I don't mean literally. Oh, great, my son has you believing I ripped out his sister's heart and now I tell you I suffocated his father. No, I mean all the burdens. We just got too much for him. He was always so tired. Felt as if the weight of the world was on his shoulders. He'd tell me he would see himself balancing on a fence with sanity on one side and insanity on the other. He would try to keep his balance but he knew that eventually he would fall and he was beginning to hope he would fall over to madness. That way someone would have to take care of him. What is it about me and weak men? All in all he was a fine man, you know. The one real man in my life. He just couldn't stay.

WOMAN: Sol was always ashamed of me. As if people would connect an abnormal child to an abnormal mother. She would try never to acknowledge me in public. Oh, she would dress me up and comb my hair, but once we got outside, her son was her only child. My brother would hold my hand. Taught me how to curtsy whenever he touched my elbow just so. And just how big a smile I should give to whomever had given me money.

(The BOY *puts his hands on the* GIRL*'s face and repeatedly shapes her face into a smile, each one broader than the last. He laughs and the* GIRL *silently joins him. They fall back on the bed.)*

WOMAN: A quarter feels different than a nickel and paper money would get the biggest smile of all, plus the curtsy.

SON: Sol was only doing it in the meantime. She would entertain men and support us and put a little aside for a sewing machine. An industrial sewing machine. She would be able to do her sewing at home and care for her children.

SOL: Like any good Christian mother, but—

*(*SOL *enters her former bedroom and becomes the younger* SOL *(i e, hair loose, no cigar, robe, not house dress. She is coughing and very ill. When she coughs she covers her mouth with a handkerchief; we see it stained in blood. The* BOY *guides the* GIRL *and together they help* SOL *to the bed.* SOL *tries to sit, but can't. She lies on the bed. The* GIRL *begins to softly smooth out* SOL*'s hair. The boy takes* SOL*'s hand and kisses it. There is a knock on the door.)*

SON'S VOICE: No, Sol. You can't.

SOL: We gotta eat, Baby.

*(*SOL *ushers* BOY*, who pulls* GIRL *with him to the closet.* SOL *holds onto the bed and tries to look seductive. A* MAN *enters and takes her in his arms. The* MAN *kisses* SOL *and his mouth is smeared in blood. He pushes her on the bed and wipes his mouth with the back of his hand. He takes off his belt and begins to beat* SOL. SOL *screams and her children enter. The* BOY *attacks the* MAN *and the* GIRL *throws her arms around like a windmill. The* MAN *kicks off the* BOY *and exits.* SOL *huddles with her children on the bed. Blackout. The lights come up to indicate another day.* SOL *is weaker. There is a knock on the door. The* BOY *automatically takes the* GIRL *into the closet.* SOL *cannot even stand. She sits up in bed as best she can. A drunk enters. He is too drunk to care about* SOL*'s condition. He gets into bed with her. Lights dim. The* BOY *enters the room. He stands watching the bed, the sound of sex filling his ears. The* GIRL *enters. The* BOY *takes her hand and continues watching. Blackout. The lights come up to indicate another day.* SOL *is now flat on her back, too weak to move. The* GIRL *sits playing with the brush on the floor. The* BOY *is trying to feed* SOL *some soup, but she is too weak to swallow. A knock is heard. The* BOY *takes the* GIRL *to the closet, then stops. He looks at* SOL *who is crying softly into her pillow. The* BOY *takes the brush from the* GIRL*'s hand and brushes her hair. He pinches her cheeks and takes her to the bed. He lays her down, goes to the door,*

and lets a MAN *in. The* MAN *is about to leave when he sees* SOL, *but the* BOY *guides him to the* GIRL. *The* MAN *shrugs and begins to undress. Lights fade.)*

WOMAN: No!

SON: We had to eat! Sol was dying. You were so pretty. Weren't you pretty? Didn't people give you money in the streets for being so pretty? That money bought medicine. That money bought food. You couldn't hear, you couldn't see, you couldn't speak. As the man undressed I hid under the bed. I was your voice, your moans. We were a team.

WOMAN: Some team.

SOL: Children. Let's not forget about me. I came as close to dying as I ever want to get. To be so weak that I'd have to let something like that happen right next to me, on what I thought was my deathbed. My ugly son pimping my idiot daughter. Damn, this must be hell, I thought. Seeing him slink under the bed to moan for her. You can't possibly know what hell is, Baby. I've been there and back. I'd lay there, delirious, and see my men with my daughter and my son begging for more. Is that what I looked like? Is that what I sounded like? I fell into a deep sleep where I couldn't feel or hear anything. I thought I had died. I woke up days later, hungry enough to eat anything.

(Light up on bedroom. The BOY *and the* GIRL *are sleeping in bed.* SOL *slowly sits up. She is cured. She gets out of bed and helps herself to the table. She begins to eat some bread when a knock is heard.* SOL *hurries as best she can to the bed and tries to wake her children to no avail. She gives up and stands by the foot of the bed. She throws her hair back seductively. A* MAN *enters and goes to* SOL, *then looks at the bed and heads for* GIRL.*)*

SOL: What the hell do you think you're doing?

MAN: Don't I have a choice in the matter?

SOL: No, you have no choice. Get the hell out!

*(*MAN *exits.)*

SOL: I was blinded by my rage. I wanted to hurt him. I wanted him to come crawling back to me. I...I quite suddenly became riveted in place. And I knew that all I had to do was write his name on a piece of paper and swallow it and he would come back. Now, I knew nothing of this before. I didn't even believe in it. But my illness let in something that would just tell me these things. And so I did it. And he did.

(The MAN *enters on his hands and knees. He kisses the hem of* SOL*'s robe. The* BOY *and the* GIRL *wake up.* SOL *gestures for them to leave. They don't.)*

SOL: Take that idiot into the closet with you right now!

(The BOY *guides the* GIRL *to the closet. They enter.* SOL *and the* MAN *lay on the bed. The lights dim. The* GIRL *comes out of the closet and stands next to the bed. The* BOY *comes out and tries to take her back in. She violently shakes him off and continues by the bed.)*

CUSTOMER: *(Voice only)* Doña Sol!

(The action stops in the bedroom. A CUSTOMER *has entered* SOL*'s consultation area on the other side of the stage. The* BOY *and the* GIRL *run into the closet.* SOL *sits up in bed.)*

CUSTOMER: Doña Sol!

SOL: Now what?

*(*SOL *shakes the* MAN *and he exits.* SOL *jumps out of bed and puts on her house dress and puts her hair up in a bun. She takes out her cigar from the house dress pocket and exits to her consultation area. Lights fade on bedroom, up on consultation area. A* CUSTOMER *sits with her back to the audience as* SOL *enters.)*

SOL: What is it now?

CUSTOMER: Oh please, Doña Sol. I need your help.

SOL: Fine, fine. Let's get on with it.

CUSTOMER: I just don't know what to do.

SOL: Evil eye, lost love. Don't you people ever get tired of the same crap?

CUSTOMER: I know that only your spiritual guidance can help me.

SOL: Yeah, yeah.

CUSTOMER: Please forgive me for coming so early.

SOL: That's just what her husband told me the last time I saw him.

CUSTOMER: But only you can help me.

*(*SOL*, who has been shuffling the cards, places them on the table.)*

SOL: Cut. You know the procedure.

*(*CUSTOMER *does.)*

SOL: Actually, I know what her problem is and I know what my solution will be; but I gotta go through all this mumbo jumbo so it will look spiritual to them.

CUSTOMER: Oh please, let me drink from your fountain of wisdom.

SOL: My fountain of wisdom, no less. Let me see. This is about your lover. His name is—

CUSTOMER: Jaime.

SOL: Who's reading these cards, you or me? He has threatened to kill himself if you don't run off with him.

CUSTOMER: What am I to do? What am I to do?

SOL: You have children. You are tied down. To a good man?

CUSTOMER: Yes.

SOL: But not exciting.

CUSTOMER: He's a good man.

SOL: Your lover will die if he has to go on sharing you.

CUSTOMER: I know I'm a sinner, Doña Sol, but please help me.

SOL: Leave your husband.

CUSTOMER: I can't. My children.

SOL: Oh yes, your children. You should have thought of that before you started your whoring.

CUSTOMER: I'm a sinner.

SOL: Leave your lover.

CUSTOMER: I can't. He'll kill himself.

SOL: People seldom kill whom they mean to kill.

(SON enters.)

SON: That's deep, Sol.

CUSTOMER: Help me, please help me, Doña Sol.

SOL: Wait until midnight. Light two candles; one red, one white. Write your husband's name on a piece of paper and your lover's on another. Put your husband's name under the white candle and your lover's under the red. And don't ever wear green. That will do it.

CUSTOMER: Oh bless you, Doña Sol.

SOL: Go now.

CUSTOMER: How much?

SOL: Whatever you think is fair.

(The CUSTOMER pays and exits.)

SON: Don't wear green?

SOL: A little fashion guidance with their spiritual consultation.

SON: Don't start losing respect for your gift, Sol.

SOL: I never asked for and I never had too much respect for it in the first place. Great gift. Will it tell me the numbers for Tuesday or help me pick the winning horse at the track, no; just helps me meddle. This is a gift? Of this I should be proud?

(WOMAN enters.)

WOMAN: There were a few miracles along the way.

SON: I always have nightmares about them. Of drowning. Of being in a room where the walls, floor and ceiling are water. I swim to the top because I see light there and just where the surface is, just where I might breathe again is a sheet of glass. I can't get through. I can see the air, but I can't have any. I begin to crash my head against the glass. I'm cutting my head by pounding it against the glass and all I'm doing is making little cracks in the glass. Not enough air. Not nearly enough. And then I'm in front of my bathroom mirror pulling little pieces of glass out of my face. My hideous face. That's why I'm so ugly. That's why only Sol loves me.

SOL: Come to bed, Baby.

SON: I can't. My nightmare.

SOL: You won't sleep. I guarantee it. Come to bed.

(They exit. SON goes to the back, but is still seen. SOL enters her Past bedroom. The BOY and the GIRL enter from the closet.)

WOMAN: Ladies and gentlemen—

SOL: *(Becoming the younger SOL)* Another part padder.

WOMAN: Doña Sol's first miracle!

SON: I can't focus.

WOMAN: Try.

SON: I can't.

SOL: Actually my first miracle was that I didn't kill both of them.

(The BOY is sucking his thumb with his head in the GIRL's lap. The GIRL is softly brushing her hair. Whereas before the brush was a toy, now it is an object of pleasure. SOL enters.)

BOY: Cigar.

(SOL removes it and puts it in the pocket of her house dress. She is now in her robe.)

SOL: Sorry.

(SOL sits at vanity table. She looks at her faces and tries to summon her seductive self. She massages her neck and shakes her hair. She reaches for her brush and sees the GIRL in her mirror, brushing her hair.)

(SOL gets up and takes the brush away from GIRL. The GIRL has a fit.)

BOY: Give it back to her. Give it back to her.

(Reluctantly, SOL does.)

SOL: Is she planning a hot date tonight? Wouldn't you rather comb Sol's hair?

BOY: No.

SOL: I am still the mother here. I still pay the bills.

BOY: You may retire now.

SOL: Or take it on the road. My idiot daughter and my ventriloquist son.

(A knock is heard. The GIRL pushes the BOY off her lap. Both GIRL and SOL rise.)

SOL: Where the hell do you think you're going?

(The BOY scrambles under the bed.)

SOL: And you? *(She grabs BOY.)*

BOY: Please, Sol.

SOL: No one understands the kind of pressure I'm under. My own flesh and blood can't fake it long enough to understand.

(SOL grabs BOY by the ankles and pulls him from under the bed. She pushes him into the closet.)

SOL: I do my own sound effects you ugly bastard!

(SOL grabs GIRL, who begins to hit her with the hair brush.)

SOL: Ouch! You get into the closet.

(The GIRL shakes her head no.)

SOL: I'm not asking you to do me a favor, I'm telling you.

(The GIRL keeps shaking her head.)

BOY: Sol, she's listening. She can hear you.

(SOL kneels and embraces the GIRL.)

SOL: My baby! It's a miracle! My baby can hear!

(The GIRL spits into SOL's face. Again the knock is heard. SOL throws the GIRL to BOY. She stamps her foot in rage. The BOY pulls the GIRL into the closet. A MAN enters and embraces SOL, whose eyes remain on the closet.)

VOICE: Doña Sol!

SOL: For Pete's fucking sake!

VOICE: Please, Doña Sol.

SOL: That's it. Can't a person recreate a few spiritual miracles in peace?

VOICE: Oh please, Doña Sol.

SOL: I'm not going.

(The BOY *and the* GIRL *come out of the closet and the* MAN *gets out of bed.)*

MAN: You've got to go, Doña Sol.

BOY: She needs your help.

SOL: I'm not getting into that old Sol drag. Uh, uh. I'm very sorry.

VOICE: Where are you, Doña Sol?

SOL: I am trying to recreate a life, if you don't mind.

(The MAN *and the* BOY *and* GIRL *drag* SOL *to the edge of her Past bedroom area.* SOL *becomes the spiritual* SOL. *The* MAN, BOY, *and* GIRL *won't cross over into the consultation area.)*

SOL: No one cares. No one gives a shit. It doesn't matter if you're tired. If you feel like you want to scream or explode or grab the thing nearest to you and start hitting people. Oh God, to be left alone. Not to hear someone come up behind you waiting to take a piece of you.

SON: Maybe if you cried more.

SOL: I'm not into those heavy dramatics. I just want to rest. Put down my burden and wipe my brow.

SON: *(Wiping her brow)* You've come so far, Doña Sol.

SOL: Yeah, and what happens when I can't get it up anymore? When my remedies and my cigars are gone?

SON: *(Putting cigar in her mouth)* You will always have me.

*(*SON *kisses* SOL.*)*

CUSTOMER: Doña Sol, this is a pleasure.

*(*SOL *sits and begins to shuffle cards. The* CUSTOMER *is a reporter.)*

SOL: As long as you're not screaming and crying and pulling your hair, you're okay. Tense. She's just a little tense. Maybe she's going through her change. Cut.

CUSTOMER: Excuse me.

SOL: My mother used to say, "Don't eat, that's the only way a man will believe you're sick."

(The CUSTOMER *takes out a pocket tape recorder.)*

CUSTOMER: I should be getting some of this down.

SOL: Wait a minute. Who the hell are you?

CUSTOMER: I'm a writer. I've come to write your life story. "Doña Sol: A Goddess for Our Times."

(The BOY and the GIRL, who are sitting on the bed, giggle.)

SOL: I'm not through with you two. I've got my eye on both of you.

CUSTOMER: Actually it's just me and the millions of your devoted fans who breathlessly await your story.

WOMAN: What a golden opportunity to recreate a life, goddess.

SOL: My story?

CUSTOMER: Major event by major event.

SOL: Well, there's really nothing much to say.

WOMAN: That used to be my line.

CUSTOMER: A simple whore brings her people to a religious climax.

SOL: I recall it as a slightly more—

CUSTOMER: How you saved your son from his sins. Freeing him to take his rightful place at your side.

SON: I'm a good boy.

SOL: I don't do interviews

SON: At least tell her I am a good boy.

CUSTOMER: Your story could give hope to so many. Won't you please share it?

SOL: Such a simple story, really. I was born to poor, but hard-working parents. My father was a house painter, my mother stayed at home with her eighteen children. Did I say eighteen children? I'm sorry. I was an only child. I married very young. My husband and I had one son. My husband was a former customer—

WOMAN: You're dating yourself.

SOL: —a former customer relations manager at a bank, when I met him. He died in a hold-up attempt only days before his only child was born.

(The SON sits on SOL's lap.)

SOL: He died a hero.

SON: Tell her I'm a good boy.

SOL: Yeah, and this one is a good boy.

CUSTOMER: And your daughter?

SOL: My what?

WOMAN: She must have you confused with another whore goddess.

CUSTOMER: There have been rumors that your son had a sister. That your daughter's beauty rivaled your own and that she had a deep, sensual moan.

SON: That she did.

(Both SOL *and* WOMAN *hit* SON.*)*

SOL: I don't know how these fantasies get started. Overdeveloped imaginations pulling away curtains to get a glimpse of a neighbor's life. Rearranging it to meet their ideal level for gossip.

CUSTOMER: They say that your daughter was killed by a jealous wife; is a nun in a small underdeveloped country; or is a vegetable hidden away in a private hospital.

SON: I like the nun one.

SOL: I have no daughter. Write that down. Spell it out for my followers.

CUSTOMER: *(To* SON*)* Well, let me put it this way, did you have a sister?

*(*SOL *and* SON *answer at once.)*

SOL: He was an only child.

SON: Yes.

SOL: My son preferred dressing as a little girl when he was a child. He was my first worshipper. He wanted so to be like his Doña Sol.

SON: I'm a good boy.

SOL: That's why he tried to become me. He was actually quite a pretty girl.

SON: I was ugly.

SOL: No, Baby. Now you're ugly, then you were pretty.

SON: I'm a good boy.

SOL: We'll see.

CUSTOMER: No daughter?

SOL: How I would have killed for a daughter. Someone beautiful and good. But you see what my lot in life was. A son who has been in and out of mental hospitals for almost twenty years. But now he's cured. That's what your book should be about. A celebration. A mother and child reunion.

SON: Tell her I'm a good boy. Tell her you're proud of me.

CUSTOMER: And what can you tell us about Doña Sol?

SON: Sol. Doña Sol is the most beautiful woman in the world. She's a saint. And she never makes fun of me. She has done so much good for people and she's got terrific legs and she—

SOL: To him, I'm a cross between Rita Hayworth and Joan of Arc.

SON: She is so good. So good that she could only have a good son. Only the best son for our Doña Sol.

SOL: You're a good boy.

SON: Tell her you respect me.

SOL: I can't, Baby. I don't.

(The CUSTOMER *exits.)*

SON: Tell her I'm a good boy.

SOL: The media's not interested .

SON: In me or you.

SOL: You're a bad boy.

WOMAN: Your second miracle, Doña Sol.

*(*SOL *walks into the Past bedroom with the* SON *screaming after.)*

SON: You're supposed to respect me! I've earned it. I've worked too hard for just a pat on the fucking head. You owe me, Lady. You took out my heart, you owe me. Why do I have to beg to hear it from you? Haven't I've been good enough?

SOL: I'm not supposed to hear him here.

SON: Just tell me I'm good enough or as good or that you're proud of me. I am not a bad person, Doña Sol.

(The WOMAN *leads the* SON *off.)*

WOMAN: Come on.

SON: There are worse people than me in the world. Why can't she respect me? She respects you. She respects you because you hit her and you spat on her. I was a good boy.

SOL: Yes, he was.

(As the SON *is led off)*

SON: Why wasn't I good enough? Why was I never the best?

(Lights out in the consultation area. The BOY *and the* GIRL *enter.)*

SOL: Not yet. I...I can't focus.

(The BOY *and the* GIRL *go quietly back into the closet.)*

SOL: I do love him, but no, I don't respect him. I cannot respect him.

(SOL goes to the closet and opens the door.)

SOL: Come out you little brats, come help doña Sol hang herself.

(The BOY and the GIRL enter. The BOY sits on the floor by the bed; the GIRL sits on it. They are holding hands. The BOY whispers in the GIRL's ear.)

SOL: He had found an audience; how could I take that away from him? Life continued as always. I working diligently towards my industrial sewing machine and my obedient children at my feet.

SON: *(Voice only)* Maybe I don't love you, Doña Sol. Maybe I don't respect you either.

SOL: Will someone shut him up!

(Pause)

BOY: Go ahead, Doña Sol.

SOL: I can't focus.

BOY: Yes you can.

(SOL embraces her children.)

SOL: If you ever understand any of this explain it to me.

BOY: People will believe what they want to believe.

SOL: I've taught him well. After my first miracle my whole way of speaking had to change. It had never occurred to me how many times I had referred to her as—

WOMAN: The Idiot.

SOL: The Idiot. But now she could hear me. Could hear me through the door doing what she wanted to do. She could hear me well enough to find and attack me. She could hear me well enough to take my son away.

(A knock is heard. The GIRL goes to vanity, looks into the glass, and brushes her hair. When SOL reaches vanity, GIRL breaks away and stands by the bed in the same pose SOL has assumed whenever there has been a knock at the door. GIRL stares at the door.)

SOL: She can see.

BOY: It's our turn now.

SOL: This is not a game. What, did one of you stop being an idiot and the other become one?

(A MAN enters. GIRL curtsies, turns, and smiles at SOL. The BOY opens the closet door.)

BOY: Come on, Sol.

(SOL goes to the door and slams it.)

SOL: You must be goddamn crazy!

(SOL pounces on the GIRL. The MAN intercedes and forces SOL into the closet.)

SOL: No! You've got the wrong one. She's broken. She's a dummy who sits on her brother's knee.

(SOL is in the closet. The BOY scurries under the bed. Lights out on bed. Lights up on closet interior. SOL sits crouched in closet.)

VOICE: Doña Sol, Doña Sol.

SOL: Go to hell!

(VOICE fades. SOL remains in closet.)

SOL: I'm sitting there feeling so trapped and I know that even after I leave this closet I'll still feel trapped. And worthless. To be replaced, we all expect; but to be replaced by the one next to you. I'd leave. Find a nice man to support me. Someone who could love a woman, not a child. If such a man exists.

(Lights out on closet. Lights up in bedroom. SOL enters. GIRL is sitting at vanity putting on SOL's make-up. SOL approaches her, decides against it, and sits by BOY on the bed.)

SOL: Maybe such a man can be created.

(WOMAN enters bedroom.)

WOMAN: Ah, yes, the seduction.

SOL: What can I give him?

WOMAN: That I haven't?

SOL: That she hasn't. That will make him mine.

WOMAN: That will take him away from me. A mother's love.

(SOL begins to rock BOY in her arms.)

SOL: A mother's love.

WOMAN: Of course first he has to want it.

SOL: I don't expect him to ask for it by name.

(WOMAN goes to GIRL and helps her apply make-up.)

SOL: If it were different, how much more patience would you have had?

(WOMAN and GIRL ignore SOL.)

SOL: You're a good boy.

BOY: Yes.

SOL: Focus.

BOY: Yes.

SOL: Stand up.

(BOY does.)

SOL: Good boy. Turn around. Good boy. Give Mami a kiss.

BOY: You're not Mami, you're Sol.

SOL: Yes, I'm Sol; but when you kiss me I'm Mami.

(BOY shyly kisses SOL. WOMAN exits.)

SOL: Good boy. I have never lied to my boy. Get me the knife on the table.

(BOY does.)

SOL: Good boy. Jump. Good boy. My beautiful son. My only son. Put back the knife. Good boy. Give it to me. Good son. Put back the knife. Obedient son. Give it to me. Perfect son. Put back the knife. Wonderful son. Give me the knife. Beautiful son. Put back the knife. Holy son. Give me the knife. Here's a kiss. Put back the knife. Give me the knife, put back the knife, give me the knife, put back the knife, give me the knife.

(The pace builds and the BOY becomes confused.)

SOL: Oh, you've cut me. It was an accident, my dearest son. You've cut your Sol. No I don't think you should see my cut. A son should never see his mother's blood. I know you didn't mean it, Baby. Give Sol a big hug.

(BOY does.)

SOL: No matter what you do Sol will always love you. And I won't tell anyone you cut me. You're a good boy.

BOY: I'm sorry.

SOL: Shh, Baby.

(GIRL comes to SOL and BOY. BOY is in SOL's arms. GIRL softly begins to brush BOY's hair.)

SOL: Leave him alone.

(GIRL continues. BOY looks up and smiles at GIRL.)

SOL: Close your eyes. Close your eyes!

(BOY does.)

SOL: Good boy. Now you can't see how you hurt Sol.

(Lights out. Lights up on an empty piece of stage. SON *appears with a knife.* WOMAN *walks ahead of him. Knocks are heard and one by one men appear.* SON *kills them all until he is right behind* WOMAN. *She turns around.* SON *gives her the knife and kneels in front of her.)*

SON: I've brought you back your heart.

(Lights out. Lights up on bedroom. A knock is heard. GIRL *stands by the bed.* BOY *opens the closet for* SOL.*)*

VOICE: Doña Sol, please Doña Sol. Aren't you back yet?

SOL: *(To* BOY*)* You're a bad boy. *(Turning into older* SOL*)* You're an ugly son. You go ahead without me. I know how this part turns out.

*(*SOL *exits.* BOY *runs under the bed.* SOL *enters the consultation area. The* WOMAN *is the voice that called her.)*

SOL: *(Taken aback.)* It may be a little late for you. I don't bring back the dead.

WOMAN: Oh, please, Doña Sol. I have a problem.

SOL: Can your sarcasm.

WOMAN: How can you listen to such bullshit every day? Doesn't your mind begin to rot? You gave up whoring for this?

SOL: I was retired. I'm more comfortable facing strangers in that chair.

WOMAN: You are.

SOL: You shouldn't have called me. I was about to perform a miracle. My third miracle; one I prayed and worked for.

WOMAN: Your last miracle. You still have trouble focusing?

SOL: Sometimes.

WOMAN: And he does too?

SOL: And he does, too.

WOMAN: Like mother, like son.

SOL: Like daughter.

WOMAN: You've got a real selective memory about having a daughter. Not that I blame you. Were you ever afraid you would lose your sight, your hearing? That you'd wake up one morning and want to scream, but no sound would come out? Did you wonder if I was becoming you, were you doomed to become me? You're not shuffling, Doña Sol.

SOL: You're making fun of me.

WOMAN: Not anymore. Tell me, how did it feel to lie there in the bed next to your daughter who was doing what you couldn't do?

SOL: I'm not up to a heavy confrontation scene right now, Baby.

WOMAN: Don't call me Baby!

SOL: I must have been one damned fine mother. Both my children want to follow in my footsteps.

WOMAN: I wanted to be a whore.

SOL: Yeah? And he wanted to perform miracles.

WOMAN: *(Sarcastically)* Poor Sol.

SOL: We were coming home from church once. Just you and me. Your brother was in the hospital with his weak heart.

WOMAN: Oh please, he never had a weak heart.

SOL: All right then. I lied. He was home asleep. The little mother fucker had probably gone to an earlier Mass. The church was in the town square. As we were leaving I noticed an army truck parked on the other side of the square.

WOMAN: And soldiers.

SOL: My sewing machine was about to become a reality. But these soldiers were pulling women into the back of the truck. Whores. All whores to the army base for a medical. Preventive maintenance against social diseases. Women I knew were being dragged crying and cursing into the truck. And the town which had been in church with me just seconds before were identifying the town whores. "There's one! You missed one. Don't let that one get away."

WOMAN: That's the only time you ever held my hand in public. A mother could never be a whore.

SOL: I tried to hurry. To the hospital to visit your brother.

(The WOMAN *turns her back on* SOL.*)*

SOL: All right, home before someone spotted me. And then a woman whose hand she had offered me when the priest had asked us to greet our neighbors; the very same hand I had shaken, was now pointing at me. "Whore!" You were grabbed from my side and I was dragged through the square, past my sainted neighbors to the truck. I screamed. I begged. "I am not a whore. I am a mother. I am a seamstress." But no, I was thrown into the truck with the other seamstresses.

(The WOMAN *comes behind* SOL *and gently brushes her hair.)*

SOL: You know the last thing I did was? Just before the truck pulled out I saw a woman who was being dragged by soldiers. She wasn't a whore. She was the victim of a woman's jealousy. I stood up in the truck and I pointed at her. "She's not one of us. She's not a whore like me." They let her go.

"Come on," I added, "The sooner your men look up my snatch the sooner you get to use it." The soldiers left her and got into the truck. The last thing I saw was you, wandering around the square and bumping into people.

WOMAN: What happened to you?

SOL: The usual. Deliced. Scrubbed raw with steel wool. Shots until you started throwing up and shots to make you stop.

WOMAN: That's what you saved that woman from?

SOL: Hell, she wasn't a working girl; like us.

WOMAN: Like us. I hate myself for this, but I have to hear it from you. I was better than you, wasn't I?

SOL: Why do you think I killed you?

(WOMAN kneels and puts her head in SOL's lap. SOL realizes her hair is down.)

SOL: I never wear my hair down here.

WOMAN: You have to go back.

SOL: I can't.

WOMAN: You have to go back. How much do I owe you.

SOL: Whatever you think is fair.

(WOMAN stays and SOL exits. Lights out on consultation area. Lights up on bedroom. SOL puts on a robe. A knock is heard.)

SOL: Jesus Christ! What have you got? A conveyor belt?

(BOY leads SOL to closet. GIRL stands by the bed. SOL enters closet. MAN enters.)

GIRL: *(To BOY)* You too.

SOL: *(From closet)* Bingo.

GIRL: You, too. Hurry up.

(GIRL curtsies to MAN.)

BOY: You need me.

GIRL: Not anymore.

BOY: I'm your voice.

GIRL: Not anymore.

BOY: I'm a good voice.

GIRL: Mine is better.

BOY: I'm a good voice. I'm a good voice. I'm a good boy.

GIRL: I'm better.

MAN: Yes, she is.

GIRL: Go away.

*(*MAN *approaches* BOY. SOL *enters from closet and shields* BOY. MAN *steps back.* SOL *hugs* BOY.*)*

SOL: *(To* BOY*)* Go now.

*(*BOY *exits off stage.* SOL *goes to bed.)*

SOL: Never send a man to do a boy's job.

*(*SOL *reaches under the bed and pulls out* SON*, putting him where* BOY *was.)*

SOL: This is what happened. This is what you have to face.

*(*SOL *returns to closet.)*

GIRL: I'm better.

SON: She was better.

*(*MAN *opens closet.* SON *enters. Lights out in bedroom, up in closet.)*

SON: Why is she better?

SOL: There, there Baby.

SON: Make me good enough, Sol.

SOL: You have a weak heart.

SON: I'm ugly.

SOL: You need a stronger heart.

SON: I need me.

SOL: Focus, Baby.

SON: No, Sol, please.

*(*SOL *begins to kiss* SON*'s face.)*

SOL: If you only had a stronger heart. Then you would be with me forever.

SON: This is not how it happened.

SOL: It's close enough.

*(*SON *is returning* SOL*'s kisses.)*

SON: Yes, it's close enough.

SOL: Will you avenge my honor? Will you be a good boy?

SON: Yes.

SOL: I'm proud of you, Baby. Doña Sol respects you.

(GIRL sits up in bed. She goes to vanity and sits, brushing her hair. SON enters and picks up knife. He takes a few tentative steps toward the GIRL and then drops to his knees. SOL enters. She takes the knife from SON and approaches GIRL as lights fade.)

SOL: What is it about me and weak men?

(Music from the first scene is heard.)

#1: Murderer.

#2: Whore, come out and pay for your sins.

#3: She has shamed us.

(Lights up on closet door. SOL leaves it wearing the bloodstained robe she wore in the beginning. The bedroom is empty. SOL puts her housedress over her robe and puts her hair up. She looks in her pocket for her cigar but can't find it. She carries the knife. In the consultation area, a match is lit and a dim red light appears. SOL enters consultation area as lights fade on closet. SON is sitting in SOL's place, where he is shuffling her cards and smoking her cigar.)

SON: You're having trouble...you're having trouble with your son.

SOL: Yes.

SON: He lies.

SOL: All the time.

SON: Not all the time. Cut.

(SOL raises the knife, but puts it on the table. She cuts the cards.)

SOL: There will be no fee for your visit, Doña Sol. Consider it professional courtesy, Baby.

SOL: My son lies.

SON: What does he lie about?

SOL: I'm not sure but everything he says can't be true.

SON: No, of course not.

SOL: What can I do to cure his lying?

SON: Actually, the way I see it, Baby, what I have to cure is your hearing. So you'll only hear the truth.

SOL: Tell me how. I need your help, Don Son.

SON: I need a moan here, Baby.

(SOL moans.)

SON: Good. Now I want you to give me a heart. A strong, healthy heart to replace my weak one. Do you have a strong heart?

SOL: Yes.

SON: Good. Bring it to me wrapped in silk and I will cure your son. Your cards look very favorable. Things are beginning to look up for you. No more evil eyes, no more cigars, no more moans. Moan for me, Baby.

(SOL whimpers.)

SON: I see truth right around the corner for you. Your honesty will be well rewarded. Go now.

(SOL rises as BOY enters. SON hands BOY knife.)

SON: Don't forget. Your heart wrapped in silk.

BOY: She'll bring it right over.

(SOL begins to walk out, with BOY following her. Her head is held high. The voices of her worshippers eerily echo in the background. Before she exits she turns and faces SON.)

SOL: Oh, and one last thing, Don Son. Don't wear green.

(Blackout)

END OF PLAY

TRAFFICKING IN BROKEN HEARTS

ORIGINAL PRODUCTION

TRAFFICKING IN BROKEN HEARTS was first produced by Bailiwick Repertory, Chicago IL during the 1992 Pride Performance Series.

TRAFFICKING IN BROKEN HEARTS was subsequently produced in New York in 1994 by the Atlantic Theater Company (Neil Pepe, Artistic Director; Joshua Lehrer, Managing Director). The cast and creative contributors were:

PAPO .... Giancarlo Esposito
BRIAN .... Neil Pepe
BOBBY .... Anthony Rapp

Director .... Anna D Shapiro
Set and light design .... Kevin Rigdon
Costume design .... Laura Cunningham
Sound design .... One Dream Sound
Original music .... Max Shapiro
Fight choreography .... Rick Sordelet

CHARACTERS AND SETTING

PAPO, *a hustler, 26 years old*
BRIAN, *a lawyer, 26 years old*
BOBBY, *a runaway, 16 years old*

Assorted voices that will represent the voices of New York

The play takes place primarily in the 42nd Street area of New York City.

(At rise: From the darkness neon begins to turn on and off. Voices are heard, some dirty talk, some high-pitched laughter. Drugs and sex are offered. All we see are flashing lights. The lights slowly come up to a dim. A fight is happening somewhere, a siren, someone asking for spare change while another voice is demanding that gentlemen drop their quarters. We see the facade of a peep show. PAPO, *his back to the audience, stretches and yawns. He opens his pants and positions his cock to maximum advantage. He clears his throat and spits. He leans against the peep show facade. Lights begin to dim.)*

PAPO: Hey, you wanna see a movie?

(Blackout)

(A third of the stage is lit.)

PAPO: The first time I walked down Forty-second Street I got scared and turned back. A woman lifted her skirt and started pissing and two cops were standing right there and they didn't do anything. She wasn't wearing panties and she was ugly. I turn around and walk back. I didn't go back for a while.

(Second third is lit. BRIAN *at work. Sitting behind a desk he places a call. Music under.)*

BRIAN: Hello.

VOICE 1: Card number, please.

*(*BRIAN *fumbles in pocket for wallet. He removes a card.)*

BRIAN: Uh, 0655182.

VOICE 1: Thank you. Go ahead.

BRIAN: Hello.

VOICE 2: Hi.

BRIAN: Hi.

VOICE 2: *(Pause)* You got a real sexy voice.

BRIAN: You too. Can you tell me what you look like?

VOICE 2: Sure. I'm six feet tall, 180, body builder, 9 inches.

BRIAN: Sounds good.

VOICE 2: What are you in the mood for today?

BRIAN: I just want to hear your voice.

VOICE 2: You want me to talk dirty to you?

BRIAN: No, just talk to me.

VOICE 2: Look, what scene do you want?

(The music builds. Hard. Hypnotic. VOICE 2 *fades and* BRIAN *will speak but won't be heard over the music.* BRIAN*'s phone receiver exchanges hands and his right hand goes under his desk. He opens his pants and begins to masturbate. The music becomes louder and* BRIAN *is sweating. He moans and trembles as he comes. A second after he does a light from an open doorway appears on him. He freezes. Music stops.)*

SECRETARY'S VOICE: They're waiting for you in the conference room, Mr Ritter.

BRIAN: Tell them I'll be right in.

(Light from doorway disappears.)

VOICE 2: Are you still there? Hello.

*(*BRIAN *hangs up. He pulls a handkerchief from his pocket and cleans himself.)*

(Last third of the stage is lit. BOBBY *is sitting on the floor, hugging himself and crying.)*

BOBBY: Why do you want to marry her, Reggie? What's the matter with me? What's the matter with me?

(42nd Street peep show. PAPO *is leaning against the front. Enter* BRIAN *from off stage. He slows down in front of peep show. He enters.* PAPO *waits a couple of seconds then follows.* BRIAN *is walking past the magazines. He stops to flip through one.* PAPO *reaches in front of him to get one.)*

PAPO: 'Scuse me.

*(*BRIAN *looks at* PAPO *out of the corner of his eye.* PAPO *brushes past him on the way to the booths.* BRIAN *waits a couple of seconds then fumbles, putting magazine back.* BRIAN *enters the booth area and pretends to read the display cards on the different booths.)*

PAPO: Psst.

*(*BRIAN *looks in the booth next to him where the door is ajar.* PAPO *is inside booth, playing with himself through his pants.)*

PAPO: Hey man, you wanna see a movie?

*(*BRIAN *stands, watching as* PAPO *begins to unfasten his pants.)*

MAN'S VOICE: Let's drop some quarters, gentlemen.

*(*PAPO *gestures with his head for* BRIAN *to come in.* BRIAN *is frozen in place.)*

PAPO: C'mon man. I ain't giving no fucking free show.

BRIAN: The sign says one person per booth. What if they catch us?

PAPO: Nobody pays attention to that.

(BRIAN *looks both ways and quickly enters the booth.)*

PAPO: You got some quarters, man? You gotta drop some quarters in the machine else we can't close the door.

(BRIAN *begins to look through his pockets.)*

BRIAN: Yeah, I got a couple.

PAPO: Well, drop 'em in.

(BRIAN *does. The lights go out in the booth and a loop begins to play. They are standing in front of the screen so the film images are on their faces.* PAPO *leans against the wall, still massaging himself.)*

PAPO: Go ahead and touch it. It ain't gonna bite you.

(PAPO *reaches over and grabs one of* BRIAN*'s hands. He places it over his crotch and moves it up and down.)*

PAPO: You got some money?

BRIAN: Uh-huh.

PAPO: Okay then.

(BRIAN *awkwardly grabs* PAPO *and tries to kiss him.* PAPO *pushes him off.)*

PAPO: Look man, I don't kiss no faggots.

BRIAN: Aren't you a faggot?

PAPO: No dickface, I'm a hustler. Look, you got some money, right?

BRIAN: Yeah.

PAPO: Okay, gimme twenty.

BRIAN: What for?

PAPO: To go down on me.

BRIAN: I don't know if I want to do that.

MAN'S VOICE: Let's drop some quarters, gentlemen.

(BRIAN *deposits another quarter.)*

PAPO: Not you. When the lights go up that's when you put in another quarter.

BRIAN: I'm sorry. Look, I've never done this before.

PAPO: Yeah, sure. It's still twenty. No discounts.

BRIAN: Can I kiss you?

PAPO: I told you, I don't kiss no faggots.

*(*BRIAN *shrugs helplessly and turns to leave.* PAPO *presses against him. He begins feeling him up, looking for his wallet.)*

PAPO: Hey c'mon, man. Relax.

BRIAN: Do you have someplace else we can go?

*(*PAPO *does not find a wallet in* BRIAN*'s pants.)*

PAPO: That would be more money.

BRIAN: That's okay.

PAPO: Man, you don't have any money. Don't be fucking bullshitting me.

(Lights come up in booth.)

BRIAN: Yes I do.

PAPO: Yeah? Show me.

*(*BRIAN *is about to reach for his money when a banging is heard on their booth door.)*

MAN'S VOICE: Let's drop some quarters in there.

PAPO: *(Under his breath)* Fuck you.

BRIAN: I don't have any more quarters.

PAPO: Great. *(He reaches into his pocket and pulls one out.)* You owe me a quarter, mother fucker. *(He deposits it.)* Let me go out first. I'll meet you outside then I'll take you to my room.

BRIAN: Okay.

PAPO: Hey man, you owe me a quarter.

*(*PAPO *exits.* BRIAN *touches the screen. Outside* PAPO *is waiting.* BRIAN *comes out of the peep show.)*

BRIAN: I got more change from a man in there. Here's your quarter.

PAPO: Yeah, look, it'll be fifty for me and ten dollars for the room.

BRIAN: I haven't got much time left.

PAPO: Don't worry, it won't take much time.

BRIAN: Maybe we should leave it for another time.

PAPO: You ain't got the money, right? Goddamn, fucking queer.

BRIAN: Please be quiet. No, I got it. It's right here. *(He takes his wallet from his jacket pocket but when he looks inside he only finds a ten.)* I'm sorry but all I have is a ten.

PAPO: Yeah, well you owe me that for the feel you copped in the booth.

BRIAN: Look, I got a credit card. I could buy you something.

PAPO: I don't want nothing. Fuck the credit card. What you gonna buy me?

BRIAN: I don't know. There's a clothing store over there, pick something.

PAPO: And you buy it for me?

(They approach store.)

PAPO: How about that suit?

BRIAN: That's a hundred and twenty-five.

PAPO: Oh yeah.

BRIAN: How about that sweater?

PAPO: That's sixty-five.

BRIAN: It'll look good on you.

PAPO: So will the suit, man.

BRIAN: Wait here.

*(*BRIAN *enters shop. Lights fade. Up on flophouse.* BRIAN *and* PAPO *enter.* PAPO *is admiring his sweater.)*

BRIAN: Where's the washroom?

PAPO: This fucking sweater is ace.

BRIAN: Where can we clean up?

PAPO: Right there in the sink. They's supposed to give you a little soap and a towel but they won't if you don't ask for it.

BRIAN: Look.

PAPO: Papo.

BRIAN: Yeah, Papo. I have never done this before. With any man. Ever. I just want to be safe.

PAPO: Well, you shouldn't a bought me the sweater first, but it's okay. A lot of guys would have gotten the sweater and skipped but not me. I'll treat you right.

BRIAN: I don't want to get a disease.

PAPO: Excuse me?

BRIAN: I don't know where you've been and I know that's none of my business; but I don't want to die—

PAPO: Hey man, you think I got AIDS?

BRIAN: I'm not saying you do. I'm just saying—

PAPO: I ain't no fucking leper.

BRIAN: I've waited this long I can wait until they find a cure.

PAPO: So fucking wait.

BRIAN: Are you healthy?

PAPO: Jesus Christ, you wanna fucking note from my mother?

BRIAN: I'm afraid.

PAPO: Well look, what the fuck do you want me to do?

BRIAN: I'm afraid.

PAPO: Look, what do you want to do? Do you wanna jerk off?

BRIAN: I don't have to buy you a sweater so I can jerk myself off.

PAPO: Lissen, I ain't got all day and you ain't got all day; so what is it you want?

BRIAN: Just be a little patient. I've never done this before.

PAPO: Yeah yeah, sure sure.

BRIAN: Please don't ruin it for me.

PAPO: What the fuck am I doing? You're the one looking at me like an open sore or something.

BRIAN: I'm afraid to touch you. I'm becoming so obsessed with sex that I'm suffocating. I walk down Forty-second Street and I can't breathe.

PAPO: You ain't missing much.

BRIAN: I'm beginning to fantasize at work.

PAPO: Hey, fucking ease up. Look, I'm clean. You ain't gonna catch nothing from me. I use these. *(He throws a package of condoms on the bed.)*

BRIAN: Great.

PAPO: Let's get this show on the road. I'll pop your cherry and you'll feel like a new man.

*(*PAPO *carefully takes off his sweater and folds it neatly.* BRIAN *picks up the package of condoms.)*

BRIAN: I am trusting my life to a piece of rubber that is thin enough to read through.

PAPO: C'mon, mother fucker. They're tropical colors no less.

BRIAN: I can't. I want to, but I can't.

(PAPO stares at him.)

PAPO: Fine. Fuck you, too. But I am keeping this sweater.

BRIAN: Don't be mad.

PAPO: Hey, of course not. But lissen, I better not see you on the deuce again 'cause sweater or no sweater I'll kick your mother-fucking ass in.

BRIAN: Don't be that way.

PAPO: Come telling me I'm a fucking walking den of AIDS. What, you work for the *Post,* mother fucker?

BRIAN: Papo, can I just hold you.

PAPO: No.

BRIAN: I just want to feel you next to me.

PAPO: *(Relenting)* Fuck you.

(BRIAN tentatively approaches PAPO. PAPO smirks, but lets himself be hugged.)

PAPO: Shit, it was an expensive sweater.

(BRIAN begins to caress PAPO, who slowly begins to respond.)

PAPO: Look, mother fucker—

BRIAN: Brian.

PAPO: Brian. You ain't gonna catch that shit from me. I'm clean. Really. No tracks. Look at my arms.

BRIAN: Just hold me.

PAPO: You a virgin, right? I never met a fucking virgin before.

BRIAN: If I'm fucking I can't be a virgin.

PAPO: You know what I fucking mean.

(PAPO and BRIAN begin to kiss. PAPO begins to undress BRIAN, who panics and tries to break free. PAPO holds him. BRIAN pushes him, breaks free, and runs out. PAPO follows him. On the street.)

PAPO: C'mon back, man. You still got some time left.

BRIAN: You weren't supposed to do that.

PAPO: Okay. Okay.

BRIAN: I know where you were heading.

PAPO: Jesus fucking Christ. I'm sorry I touched you. I thought that's what you paid me for.

BRIAN: Lower your voice.

PAPO: Look, you turn me on. Not many tricks do that. I gotta fake it with most of 'em. But you, look. *(He points to his crotch.)* I don't wear underwears so I know when something is fucking getting to me.

(BRIAN is panic stricken. He walks away from PAPO and pretends to look in a store window. PAPO follows him.)

PAPO: What's the matter?

BRIAN: Will you cover that?

PAPO: C'mon. Nobody gives a fuck.

(BRIAN walks away, PAPO follows.)

PAPO: Man, you don't want to see it, you don't want to touch it. Get yourself a fucking woman.

(BRIAN tries to stretch PAPO's sweater down to cover his crotch.)

PAPO: Hey, watch it with the fucking sweater.

BRIAN: Uh, look, I thought it was the right time for me but I guess it's not.

PAPO: Hey c'mon. There's no mother-fucking contest going on. We ain't out to break a speed limit or shit like that.

BRIAN: Papo, I am a twenty-six-year-old virgin.

PAPO: You're twenty-six? You look older.

BRIAN: There are not too many of us out there.

PAPO: It's probably 'cause of the fucking suit and tie.

BRIAN: Look, I've got to go.

PAPO: You wanna meet again or something?

BRIAN: I'm...I'm not ready.

PAPO: Give you a discount. I could use some pants to go with this sweater.

BRIAN: And buy yourself some underwear. People are staring at us.

PAPO: Fuck 'em. You wanna get back together again?

BRIAN: I have to get back to work.

PAPO: Hey, I'm not good enough for you, faggot.

(BRIAN walks away. PAPO follows.)

PAPO: Look, I'm sorry. I'm sorry. My mouth is like on automatic pilot.

(BRIAN grabs PAPO's hand and shakes it.)

BRIAN: Goodbye and good luck.

(BRIAN hurriedly crosses the street.)

PAPO: Yeah, you too.

*(*PAPO *waits for a bit and then follows* BRIAN *to where he works.* BRIAN *rushes into the building not knowing he has been followed.* PAPO *smiles at the building.)*

(Lights up on BOBBY*, who is packing a knapsack full of panties.)*

BOBBY: Dear Reggie, thanks a lot for telling me yourself that you were gonna get married. It meant a whole lot to me that you called even though Mom and Dad were trying to keep it a secret. We both know how they are. Reggie, I think you are making a big mistake. There is no way this Lisa can love you the way I love you and no way you can love her the way you love your Baby. I'm going to save you, Reggie, before you make the worst mistake of our lives. Love, Baby.

(Lights up on PAPO *sitting at a table, drinking coffee.)*

PAPO: I always take a coffee at Blimpie's on Forty-second off Eighth. Right across the street from Port Authority. Pick up some change from the Jersey crowd. I used to hang out at Playland next to the old Anco Theatre, but fuck, the crowd there just kept getting younger and younger. Fucking Menudo convention. One of those snot-nosed little bastards tried to charge me. Waving his skinny ass in my face and then tells me "forty bucks". I broke his head. They don't want me at Playland no more. Fuck 'em. I don't care. I'm here for the duration.

(Lights come up on BOBBY*, who is holding a carving knife.* PAPO *remains lit, drinking his coffee silently.)*

BOBBY: No, not a whole set of knives. I think all my sister-in-law needs is a carving knife. The whole family is getting together for her birthday and I'm always giving her clothes and stuff so I figured this year I'd give her something for the house. She likes cooking so I'm sure she'll be able to utilize it. My sister-in-law really is gonna be surprised. I think mine is gonna be the best gift of all.

(Lights out on BOBBY*.)*

PAPO: And anyways right outside of Playland there's this girl preaching to everybody with a mother-fuckin' bullhorn. Yeah, that bitch. Goddamn. It's like, is Jesus Christ deaf?

(Lights up on BRIAN*. He is at his desk, lost in thought. The phone on his desk rings seven times without any sign of* BRIAN *hearing it. After the phone has stopped ringing there is a pause,* BRIAN *suddenly talks into the intercom.)*

BRIAN: Did the phone just ring?

PAPO: After I recharge my batteries at Blimpie's I head to P A. You gotta be careful though 'cause they put mothe-fucking cops everywhere. Keep moving and keep looking at the schedule so it looks like you got someplace to go. I once got pinched after I sucked a cop dry. Hell, yes! He starts in to read me my mother-fucking rights and I looked at that mother fucker and I started yelling "Rape" and he got nervous and he left.

(Lights up. PAPO *and* BOBBY *meet—the men's room at the Port Authority, five p m on Friday.* BOBBY *looks like what he is, lost. He is wearing a jacket that is too hot for the weather and carrying a knapsack. In his right hand he carries the knife in a brown paper bag. He is hot and tired. He squats down on the floor and puts his knapsack between his legs and the paper bag on top of it. He is removing his jacket when* PAPO *enters and walks right into him.)*

PAPO: Hey mother fucker, you couldn't find someplace else to park?

BOBBY: You bumped into me.

*(*PAPO *does not listen and continues walking.)*

BOBBY: You did.

*(*PAPO *has walked down the length of the stalls and returns. He is upset. Again he bumps into* BOBBY*.)*

PAPO: Goddamn it, kid. Get the fuck outta my way.

BOBBY: You bumped into me.

PAPO: What?

BOBBY: Last time too.

*(*PAPO *grabs* BOBBY*'s face.)*

PAPO: If I see you again I'm gonna kick your fuckin' ass in.

(Someone clears his throat in the last stall. PAPO *releases* BOBBY *and washes his hands.)*

VOICE: Psst.

BOBBY: What's that?

PAPO: Why don't you go over there and find out, cunt?

VOICE: Psst, hey kid.

PAPO: He means you, white boy.

BOBBY: He dropped some money.

PAPO: No, fool, he's makin' an offer you ain't gonna refuse.

BOBBY: I'm hungry.

PAPO: Tell him that. Maybe the mother fucker will buy you dinner.

BOBBY: I spent all my money on a gift.

VOICE: Psst.

BOBBY: You wanna see?

PAPO: Show it to the guy with the leak.

BOBBY: What do I have to do for the money?

PAPO: Nothing you haven't done before, only now some fool mother fucker's gonna pay to help.

BOBBY: I could use the money.

PAPO: So go ahead.

BOBBY: Can I?

PAPO: Hey faggot, I ain't your father.

(BOBBY begins to inch toward the stall.)

BOBBY: I'm sorry I bumped into you.

(PAPO watches BOBBY's slow progress in the mirror.)

PAPO: Oh, what the hell.

(PAPO grabs BOBBY's arm and steers him out of the men's room.)

PAPO: Come on, Georgie, we don't want you to miss your mother-fucking bus. You know how ma gets.

BOBBY: Bobby.

PAPO: Yeah, just move it, white boy.

(Outside of the men's room)

PAPO: Let's circulate. That guy in the last stall. The one you was going to is a cop. The second you touched that twenty he was gonna pinch your lily-white ass.

BOBBY: Why would a cop wanna pinch me?

PAPO: Arrest, fool. Fuck. Straight off the mother fuckin' bus. He'd have you for soliciting and as a runaway.

BOBBY: How do you know he's a cop?

PAPO: They all wear the same fucking shoes. All the time. Like the whole fucking police force gets a discount if they all buy them. Ugly-ass shoes.

BOBBY: I'm still hungry.

PAPO: So, go earn some money, bitch. Just watch out for the shoes.

(BOBBY takes out a cigarette, lights it, and begins to smoke. PAPO immediately takes the cigarette from his mouth, throws it on the floor, and steps on it.)

PAPO: Babies don't smoke.

(He walks away; BOBBY *follows.)*

PAPO: Goodbye, Kid.

BOBBY: I'll give you my jacket if I can stay with you for a while.

PAPO: I don't want your fucking jacket.

BOBBY: I want ice cream.

PAPO: Bitch, what is your problem. Lookee here. *(He goes to trash basket and takes out a piece of paper.)* Pencil.

BOBBY: I got a pen.

PAPO: Whatever.

*(*BOBBY *reaches into his pocket and gives* PAPO *a pen.* PAPO *looks at the arrival board and writes down a number.)*

PAPO: Okay, Kid, every time you walk up to somebody you tell him this is the bus you're waiting for. He'll tell you it ain't due for hours you tell him you're waiting for your mother and you haven't got any money and you're hungry. With a face like yours, Baby, they'll buy you something. Don't go with one of them unless they show you money. First get the money then find out what you gotta do to earn it. Capiche? Keep your eyes on their shoes, too. If a cop stops you show him this piece of paper and point to the fucking sign. Then just tell him you're gonna sit down and read comic books. They should leave you the fuck alone.

BOBBY: Who am I waiting for again?

PAPO: Your mother, asshole.

BOBBY: Right. You want to wait with me?

PAPO: You are a fool. This is just pretend so the cops don't get you. Gimme back the paper. You're gonna fuck it up.

BOBBY: I won't. Honest.

PAPO: Shit. I should just let them drag you down to juvenile. Trade down there rape you ragged.

*(*BOBBY *begins to tremble. He drops his bag.)*

PAPO: Hey shithead, don't go having a fucking seizure on me. You a fucking epileptic or something?

BOBBY: I'm just hungry, Reggie. Buy me some ice cream.

PAPO: Sure, Baby, sure. They got some Howard Johnson shit on the second floor.

BOBBY: My mother's not coming to pick me up. Can I stay with you?

PAPO: What the fuck. I ain't scored and I'm horny and you're cute. Okay. One night. One. Uno.

*(*BOBBY *picks up his bag. Blackout. Light up on* BRIAN *in a cap and gown, holding a diploma. It is his graduation day.)*

DEAN'S VOICE: ...class valedictorian, Brian Ritter.

BRIAN: Esteemed professors, honored guests, fellow students—

*(*BRIAN*'s taped voice will continue but his mouth will stop moving.)*

BRIAN'S VOICE: We have before us what appears to be a horizon with no borders, no limits. Our education and our potential guarantee us entrance to—

BRIAN: To nothing. My tie is too tight. I remember I was angry because the gown wasn't long enough to hide where my mother had lowered the hem of my cousin David's "perfectly good suit, and we can't afford a new one anyway." I am the class valedictorian in a hand-me-down suit. Voted most desperate to fit in. I always knew I was different and I always hid it. Ever since my parents caught me playing doctor with a neighbor boy. They wouldn't speak to me for a week. I was dirty. I didn't exist. Sometimes I would get so crazy I would kiss my G I Joe doll. Or I would cry and stand in a corner, praying that God would make it all better. That I would be like everybody else. What kind of parents wouldn't talk to a seven-year-old child for a week? I am getting out of here. I will become a somebody. I will win my independence. I will buy my life back from you. And when I have I'll get myself a man. A life-sized G I Joe. If I can just wait. If I can go hungry just for a little while I'll be all right.

BRIAN'SP10 VOICE: ...and in closing—

BRIAN: There's no reason anyone should know. Don't make the world angry at you, Brian. Wait.

BRIAN'S VOICE: Wait.

BRIAN: Wait.

BRIAN'S VOICE: Thank you.

(Blackout. Lights up on flophouse.)

BOBBY: Why can't I stay with you? I'll sleep on the floor. You won't even know I'm here.

PAPO: That's 'cause you won't be. Go get your own room, though you'll probably get kilt by some doped-up jerk. Go home, Kid.

BOBBY: Why don't you want me?

PAPO: Oh shit, c'mon, Kid, if you're gonna start getting all pussy on me.

BOBBY: You saved my life.

PAPO: I shoulda let the cop throw you into juvenile hall.

BOBBY: They'd kill me in there.

PAPO: Man, all those Puerto Ricans and Blacks get together and they'd rip your fucking ass in half.

BOBBY: My two older brothers would rape me 'cause I was so beautiful. Ever since I was twelve. One would hold me down and the other would rape me.

PAPO: Yeah, life's a bitch.

BOBBY: They took Polaroid pictures. They would wait until my parents were gone and make me put on my mother's clothes.

PAPO: Real Norman Rockwell stuff, white boy.

BOBBY: My parents divorced when they found the pictures. Why did they do that? They sent my brothers away to a military school and me to a nut house. My father got married again. He has a little girl, a real one. Doesn't ever want me to come over. My mother puts a lock on her closet door when I'm home with her.

PAPO: Sure, stupid. She's afraid you're gonna steal her clothes.

BOBBY: I wouldn't do that.

PAPO: I was just goofing on you, Kid.

BOBBY: My brother's getting married. That's where I was supposed to be going when I got off the bus. He found somebody else. He used to call me his Baby.

PAPO: You is all a bunch of sick fucks.

BOBBY: Reggie always treated me nice. He got me a valentine once.

PAPO: I didn't know they made them for brothers. Lissen, you're a cute kid. You'll find yourself a nice rich guy who'll take care of you. You're a fine piece of blue-eyed ass, you'll do okay.

BOBBY: I want to be your wife.

PAPO: What, do I look like your brother? Is there a blue-eyed blond football player in me that I'm not seeing? Man, last night was just a freebie, don't let it go to your head. This is just too fucking stupid for words.

BOBBY: I can cook.

PAPO: Great, so can Burger King.

BOBBY: You can pimp me. You said yourself that I was a fine piece of ass. We can make a lot of money.

PAPO: I can make a lot of money.

BOBBY: Right, you can make a lot of money.

PAPO: No, forget it. That's all I need, for the fucking cops that's got it in for me already to see me pimping a little white minor.

BOBBY: I'm not a minor.

PAPO: Save it, Baby.

BOBBY: I can steal for you. *(He pulls a small radio out of his pocket.)* Look, I took this from the guy sitting next to me on the bus. For you.

PAPO: Yeah?

BOBBY: I took it right out of his pocket. I could make you a lot of money, between stealing and making tricks.

PAPO: That's turning tricks, man. You stole this? Then how come it has your name in magic marker on the back?

BOBBY: I wrote it.

PAPO: Yeah? Bullshit. Let me see the marker you used.

BOBBY: I threw it away. It was evidence.

PAPO: Right. You can't steal and you're gonna make a fucking great hustler proposing to every john you get.

BOBBY: I'm sorry, Sir.

PAPO: Don't call me Sir. I ain't your fucking father, Baby.

BOBBY: I didn't lie about cooking. I know how to cook.

PAPO: Then fucking go get yourself a job at some dago place. Go to a Greek diner and slice up some gyros.

*(*PAPO *turns to leave.* BOBBY *pulls the knife from his jacket. He stabs at* PAPO*, barely missing him.)*

PAPO: You fucking crazy?!

BOBBY: Why can't I stay with you? *(He jumps in front of the door.)*

PAPO: I don't want to have to hurt you, Kid. Don't be pulling no knives on me.

BOBBY: Call me "Baby".

*(*PAPO *tries to push* BOBBY*, who stabs wildly at him. He slashes* PAPO*'s sweater sleeve.* PAPO *falls backwards on the floor.* BOBBY *holds the knife, poised at* PAPO*'s throat.)*

BOBBY: Please call me "Baby".

PAPO: Baby.

BOBBY: I was going to Reggie's wedding. I was. I was going to stop his marriage to that imposter. It's a good thing I met you. Now I can be yours.

PAPO: Yeah, Baby. Whatever you say.

BOBBY: You're just like Reggie was, too. You can be real rough in bed but every so often you'd kiss as if you hoped I wouldn't notice. You'd kiss my eyelids. So softly. Give me a kiss, Sir.

(They kiss with the knife still at PAPO*'s throat.)*

BOBBY: I wanna do what we did last night. Whatever you want me to do. Can I call you Reggie?

PAPO: Sure.

BOBBY: And you can call me Baby. I'll make you a good wife.

*(*BOBBY *helps* PAPO *stand.)*

BOBBY: Take off your sweater, Reggie.

PAPO: My what?

BOBBY: Your sweater, Reggie.

*(*PAPO *slowly does.)*

BOBBY: I didn't hurt you, did I?

PAPO: No, it's okay. *(Pause)* Baby.

*(*BOBBY *groans.* PAPO *grabs* BOBBY *by the back of his hair and pulls him toward him, kissing him roughly on the mouth and then very gently on the eyelids.* BOBBY *is still holding the knife.* PAPO *continues to kiss him now on the neck and shoulders.* PAPO *kisses* BOBBY*'s right arm, his hand, and then kisses the blade of the knife.)*

PAPO: Give me the knife, Baby.

*(*BOBBY *gives* PAPO *the knife.)*

PAPO: Lay down.

*(*BOBBY *does. His arms reach up for* PAPO. *Blackout. Lights up outside of Peep Show.* PAPO *is hanging out as* BRIAN *comes down the street. He sees* PAPO *and tries to walk quickly by.* PAPO *sees him and chases him.)*

PAPO: Hey Brian. Brian, wait up. *(He falls in step next to him.)* Hey man, you deaf or something?

BRIAN: I thought you people never recognize customers on the street.

PAPO: Well, fuck you very much, too.

BRIAN: I'm sorry. How are you doing?

PAPO: Okay. How about you?

BRIAN: Fine. Look, I've got to run.

PAPO: Run my ass. This is your lunch break. The only place you gotta run is to a peep show.

BRIAN: Papo.

PAPO: Which is cool 'cause that's where I met you.

BRIAN: Hey, you need a couple of bucks?

PAPO: Shit, can't I talk to you without your wallet getting all itchy?

BRIAN: Sorry. What do you want?

PAPO: Well man, I see you're in the market for some action.

BRIAN: Papo.

PAPO: No strings.

BRIAN: I was kind of looking for somebody else.

PAPO: Yeah, well, fuck you.

(BRIAN *walks away.* PAPO *follows.)*

PAPO: Hey look man, I'm sorry. I haven't seen you in a while. I guess I'm jumpy, that's all. Friends?

BRIAN: Sure.

(PAPO *and* BRIAN *shake hands.)*

BRIAN: Look, I don't have much time left.

PAPO: We can just duck in here. I got some quarters.

BRIAN: How about your place?

PAPO: Uh, no. A friend is kinda staying there. A real sweet kid, a little psycho is all.

BRIAN: Why are you letting him stay?

PAPO: I don't know.

BRIAN: Is he your lover?

PAPO: Get real. Baby spends all day in panties.

BRIAN: Baby?

PAPO: The kid. The kid, okay. Hey, you jealous or something?

BRIAN: No.

PAPO: Yes you are. I sleep with this guy every night and he lets me do anything I want to him. You are jealous.

BRIAN: Papo, I really don't care.

PAPO: Yeah, I know you don't.

BRIAN: I should start getting back. I left a lot of work on my desk.

PAPO: Hey, a quickie. My treat.

BRIAN: Some other time.

PAPO: Let me walk you back then.

*(*BRIAN *stops* PAPO.*)*

BRIAN: No.

*(*PAPO *pushes* BRIAN*'s hand away.)*

PAPO: Man, I just wanna be your friend. You think you're too good for me? Fine. Fuck you. I got me a piece of sixteen-year-old white meat who'll take anything I give him. Baby treats me just fine; so fuck you. Fuck you, mother fucker.

*(*BRIAN *hurries off with* PAPO *still screaming after him.)*

PAPO: Yeah, you're too good to talk to me but you ain't too good to get my dick up your ass. Fuck you, man, just fuck you. Look, how about if I call you sometime?

(Blackout. Lights up as each person speaks.)

BRIAN: It's crazy, but I know he follows me. He thinks I don't notice, but I do. What does he want from me? He can't be in love. People like that don't fall in love and nobody falls in love with me. So what does he want?

BOBBY: I'm making him everything I ever wanted in a brother.

PAPO: *(Holding a brick)* This is where I grew up. This brick belongs to a building in the Bronx. Six-story walk-up. Fucking got asthma from living there. Going up and down those mother-fucking stairs every day. I went there a couple of years ago and the fucking building was bricked up. I hadn't been there in ten years and I expect to go back and knock on the door, tell the new people I had lived there and if I could have a fucking look around. So I go back an' it's all like fucking bricked up and I thought I should have gone back sooner.

BRIAN: Am I supposed to be the "gateway to the white world" for him?

BOBBY: And he loves me, too.

PAPO: I went back last summer and the whole place was torn down. That's when I got the brick. Sure you can tear a building down but you can't knock it down from here. *(He points to heart with brick.)*

PAPO: People don't fucking understand that. My parents live in P R now. I send them money, they don't ask questions. My baby sister lives with them. She's getting married soon.

BOBBY: I would like for us to get married. To be together for always so no one can separate us.

BRIAN: The thing is Papo doesn't know about the times I follow him. When I stand there without him seeing me and just watch him. He doesn't know the times he's helped me jerk off.

BOBBY: Don't tell Papo but I went upstate the other day. I wanted to see Reggie. I wanted to tell him it was all right. That I forgave him for getting married cause I was gonna get married, too. I'm on the bus and just as we enter into town I see Reggie outside of his car. I get off and run to him. Ronald, my other brother, was with him.

PAPO: Baby's like a pet, you know.

BOBBY: They wanted to take me back to the hospital. They say I'm sick. They say what we did together was sick and Reggie can't meet my eyes. Ronald's doing all the talking. And I tell them I got a good man, a true man. Someone who really loves me.

BRIAN: Maybe if Papo and I ran away together.

BOBBY: Ronald grabs me and I kick him in the balls. He's down. He yells for Reggie to hold me and when he does I naturally kiss him. Like always. And he looks at me and yells, "Run!" He sets me free and holds back Ronald and I hitched a ride with a trucker to the Lincoln Tunnel. I'm luckier than they are. I get to go home to someone who loves me.

(Blackout. Lights up. PAPO *is in the receptionist area of* BRIAN*'s office.)*

RECEPTIONIST: Pick-up or delivery?

PAPO: No, I'm here to see Brian.

RECEPTIONIST: Do you have an appointment with Mr. Ritter?

PAPO: Nah, it's a surprise. Just tell him Papo is here. Uh, Mr Papo Santiago. *(He can feel people looking at him. He tries to act nonchalant but finally smirks at a few people. He takes a paper cup and gets water from a water cooler. He is nervous and fidgets with the glass, accidentally puncturing it and spilling the water.)* Oh shit, I'm sorry. You got a rag or something? These little glasses are for shit.

*(*BRIAN *enters. He tries to hide his anger as he steers* PAPO *outside. He pushes him into a stairwell.)*

PAPO: Hey man, what's with you? No hello—

BRIAN: Don't you ever—

PAPO: —no nothing. Just take me off to—

BRIAN: —ever come to where I work again.

PAPO: Huh?

BRIAN: How did you find it? Did you follow me?

PAPO: Wait a second. Are you pissed off that I came to visit?

BRIAN: This is not a place for you to visit. This is where I work.

PAPO: Big fucking deal.

BRIAN: I'm serious. You are never to come—

PAPO: Fuck off, man. I just wanted to surprise you.

BRIAN: —here again. What the hell were you thinking of? Look at the way you look.

PAPO: What the hell's the matter with the way I look?

BRIAN: You look like a goddamn faggot.

*(*PAPO *punches* BRIAN.*)*

PAPO: Look, mother fucker, I come by 'cause I was gonna take you to lunch.

BRIAN: Dressed like that?

PAPO: Fuck you fuck you fuck you.

*(*BRIAN *tries to cover* PAPO*'s mouth, who pushes his hand away.* BRIAN *tries to regain his composure.)*

BRIAN: Papo...I can't receive any visitors where I work. This is not playtime, this is work.

PAPO: I fucking know that, I'm not stupid. And don't be telling me you *(He hits* BRIAN.*)* can't get any visitors 'cause everybody knows—

BRIAN: Will you just get out?

PAPO: —that you people all got your private little bars in your office for your guests. I seen that on the T V.

*(*BRIAN *reaches into his pocket and takes out his wallet. He gives* PAPO *some money.)*

BRIAN: Go buy something.

*(*PAPO *tries to jam the wallet into* BRIAN*'s mouth.)*

PAPO: Look you piece of shit I ain't no piece of shit. *(He takes the money and wipes his ass with it.)* This is what I think of your money.

BRIAN: I'm sorry. I'm sorry. Please keep your voice down.

PAPO: I went out and bought underwears, okay? Something I ain't never done for anybody.

BRIAN: Okay, okay.

PAPO: No, it's not okay. I'm sorry you're embarrassed by me, faggot.

BRIAN: Please, get out of here.

*(*PAPO *pushes* BRIAN *against the wall. He pulls an open package of underwear from his jacket. There are still two left in the package. He throws them at* BRIAN.*)*

PAPO: Here, these are yours, mother fucker.

*(*PAPO *storms out.* BRIAN *picks up his wallet, the money, and the underwear. He removes one of the briefs from the jacket and kisses it.)*

(The following scene is done with lights and sound. PAPO *is standing between two subway cars on an express train. As the lights and the sound build so do his screams. He opens his pants and struggles until he manages to rip off his underwear. Lights fade. Train sounds fade.)*

(Lights up on BRIAN *in his bedroom. He is undressing. He removes* PAPO'*s underwear from his pocket and puts a pair on. He fondles himself. He adjusts his mirror on the bureau so it can reflect on him. He lays on the bed and caresses himself, pinching his nipples.)*

BRIAN: Oh, Baby. You know that I want you so much. And you want it too, yes you do. You drive me crazy. I want to kiss every inch of your body. *(Music begins underneath.)* I've been watching you for so long. Now it's just you and me. All I want is to touch you and hold you. *(He runs his hands over his body. His eyes are shut tight.)* Oh, yes, and kiss you. *(He takes a pillow and begins to kiss it. He places another pillow between his legs.)* Nobody can see us. It's you and me, all alone. Don't we look good together? Look in the mirror. Don't we look good?

*(*BRIAN *opens his eyes.* PAPO'*s voice is heard.)*

PAPO'S VOICE: You wanna see a movie?

*(*BRIAN *sits bolt upright. He looks straight into the mirror.)*

BRIAN: I've got to get out. I've got to get out. *(He reaches madly for the phone and dials.)*

VOICE: Hello, card number please.

BRIAN: Yes, 0655182.

VOICE: Thank you. Please hold.

MAN'S VOICE: Hi.

BRIAN: I want to touch you.

MAN'S VOICE: Yeah.

BRIAN: I want you right here.

PAPO'S VOICE: You turn me on. Not many tricks do that.

BRIAN: I gotta get out. I gotta get out of here.

(He jumps from the bed and throws on a pair of slacks and a jacket. He hurriedly puts on some shoes and runs to the door. He stands frozen in place in the open doorway, unable to set foot outside of his apartment.)

BRIAN: I can't, Papo. Please, I can't.

PAPO'S VOICE: I sleep with this guy every night. He lets me do anything I want to him.

*(*BRIAN *screams out into the hallway.)*

BRIAN: Papo! *(He slams the door and collapses against it.)*

(Blackout. Lights up on flophouse. BOBBY *is wearing panties and panties are hung to dry from every available place. Enter* PAPO, *who is still upset over his turndown at* BRIAN*'s office.* BOBBY *senses trouble and tries to keep his distance.* PAPO *paces and begins to pull down the panties.)*

PAPO: I come home to a fucking laundromat.

BOBBY: I gotta put it somewhere to dry.

PAPO: They got dryers. God invented dryers, okay?

*(*BOBBY *is on his hands and knees picking up the panties.)*

BOBBY: I wash these at home, Darling. All my fine washables are done by hand.

PAPO: These are not yours. They belong to a woman. You know, a woman.

*(*PAPO *roughly grabs* BOBBY *and makes him stand. He grabs* BOBBY*'s balls.)*

PAPO: You're supposed to be a fucking guy.

*(*PAPO *pushes him aside.)*

BOBBY: I can be who I want to be, I can create myself. What's the matter, Reggie?

PAPO: Don't fucking call me Reggie! I'm confused enough as it is.

BOBBY: Are you hungry? Did you have a tough football practice? Why won't you tell Baby what's wrong?

*(*PAPO *grabs* BOBBY.*)*

PAPO: You ain't my Baby. I am not your goddamn fucking brother, see. Goddamn loony tunes. I want you out of here. You take your underwear and you make tracks back to the white world but you leave me the fuck alone.

MAN'S VOICE: Hey, you faggots wanna keep it down in there?

BOBBY: What would you do without me? You can't cook.

(PAPO sits on the bed with his head in his hands.)

PAPO: Leave me alone, man. Just leave me alone.

(BOBBY kneels next to him.)

BOBBY: I'm not a man, I'm your Baby.

(PAPO puts his arm around BOBBY's shoulder and begins to rock him.)

BOBBY: You just wait. Someday we'll get our own house, and a sheepdog, and two children.

PAPO: Fucking loony tunes.

BOBBY: And a station wagon. I'll drive you to the train station and you can catch the eight-fifteen into the city. I'll go home and get the kids off to school and clean the house and go shopping and make dinner. You know, I can really cook. *(He gets up and goes to hot plate. He returns with a pot.)* Look, I made Rice-a-roni. Your favorite, Reggie.

(PAPO begins to tremble. He knocks the pot from BOBBY's hand and begins to beat him.)

PAPO: I am not Reggie! You got that you little mother fucker? You are getting out of this place today, right now.

(BOBBY is trying to block his blows.)

BOBBY: Please, Reggie, please don't hit me. I'll do whatever you want.

PAPO: Goddamn fucking retard. *(He points to himself.)* Papo! You got that? *(He smacks him for emphasis.)* Papo!

(He throws open the door and begins to throw BOBBY's panties into the hallway. BOBBY is crying and hanging on to PAPO's leg.)

BOBBY: Please, Papo, please don't.

(Steps are heard outside the door.)

MAN'S VOICE: Hey, you wanna beat the little queer up? Fine. Just keep it down.

PAPO: This little mother fucker is outta here.

(BOBBY is still crying and wrapped around PAPO's leg.)

BOBBY: Why don't you want me, Reggie? Why? I wore the panties you wanted.

PAPO: I bought underwears!

BOBBY: You should have married me.

MAN'S VOICE: I personally don't care. I just don't want no trouble.

*(*PAPO *tries to move his leg but* BOBBY *holds on fast.)*

PAPO: It's okay, Baby.

BOBBY: Why didn't you tell me you didn't like Rice-a-roni?

MAN'S VOICE: Are you working this kid? Cute kid, you know?

PAPO: Hey man, throw me those mother fucking panties. *(*PAPO *catches them. He gently rubs* BOBBY*'s head with them.)*

BOBBY: Are you mad at me, Reggie?

PAPO: No, Baby, I'm not mad.

BOBBY: I'll do whatever you want me to do, you know that.

PAPO: Yeah, Baby, I know that.

*(*BOBBY *slowly stands and huddles under* PAPO*'s arm.)*

MAN'S VOICE: Hey look, Papo, how much for the kid?

PAPO: Baby's not for sale.

MAN'S VOICE: C'mon guy.

PAPO: But you can watch.

BOBBY: Reggie.

PAPO: Sssh.

MAN'S VOICE: How much?

PAPO: Today's rent.

MAN'S VOICE: Forget it.

PAPO: Goodnight then, mother fucker.

MAN'S VOICE: And I can watch.

PAPO: That's what I said.

MAN'S VOICE: Okay.

BOBBY: No, Reggie.

PAPO: Look, Baby, what was the name of your other fucking brother?

BOBBY: Ronald.

*(*PAPO *pushes* BOBBY *backwards on the bed. Lights go out on bed. The only light is now coming from the doorway. Fade to blackout.* BRIAN *is leaning against his desk, coffee cup in hand. He speaks to a co-worker.)*

BRIAN: I'm sorry, my mind wandered, you were saying. No, it's just personal stuff. Someone I was seeing. We're both a little too career oriented if you know what I mean. No, you couldn't possibly. I do have a life outside of this office. Just 'cause I don't spend Monday morning giving everybody a blow-by-blow account of my weekend doesn't mean I don't go out and...do stuff. Yeah, I've met somebody, but... it's over. I sort of blew my top. What I would really like to do is go away, the two of us, for a weekend maybe. Where we don't know anybody, and nobody knows us. Get to know each other a little more. Get to know each other, period. I don't know, maybe we could... there's no future in this. I want a future. I want what you have.

*(*BOBBY *is taping pictures from magazines on the wall. They are all bright and colorful.)*

PAPO: What you doing?

BOBBY: They're pretty, right?

*(*PAPO *shrugs.)*

PAPO: Where do you get the magazines?

BOBBY: From the trash.

PAPO: You don't have to be pulling no magazines from no trash. People don't have to see you like going through the fucking garbage. How do you think that makes me look.

BOBBY: Nobody saw me.

PAPO: Where do you get the tape?

*(*PAPO, *from his seated position, begins to jab his foot playfully into* BOBBY, *who continues his taping of pictures.)*

BOBBY: I took some money from your pocket.

*(*PAPO, *still playfully, jabs him a little harder.)*

PAPO: You don't even know enough to say you fucking borrowed it.

*(*BOBBY *caresses* PAPO*'s foot.)*

BOBBY: I'm sorry.

*(*PAPO *pulls his foot away.)*

BOBBY: It's kinda like my birthday.

PAPO: Today?

BOBBY: Yeah.

PAPO: Why didn't you tell me anything? I woulda...

BOBBY: Woulda what?

PAPO: Gotten you something.

BOBBY: You got me tape.

(PAPO stares at BOBBY, who continues his task. PAPO gets up and get his brick.)

PAPO: Happy birthday.

(BOBBY stares at the brick before taking it.)

PAPO: I was gonna fucking give it to you anyway. I didn't have a chance to wrap it. It's a paperweight.

(BOBBY takes the brick. He places it on a pile of pictures he has cut out.)

BOBBY: It works.

PAPO: You want to call your family or something?

BOBBY: You're my family.

PAPO: You want to go to Blimpie's?

BOBBY: I rather you brought it back home.

PAPO: Okay. *(He puts on his shoes.)* Meatball hero, right?

(BOBBY nods. He goes back to his task.)

BOBBY: And a cake.

PAPO: Where am I gonna get a fucking cake?

BOBBY: Okay, a slice of cake.

PAPO: If you ask for candles I'm a smack you.

(PAPO exits. Returns and kisses BOBBY on the top of the head.)

(Outside of peep show. BRIAN is walking by, very slowly. He sees PAPO. BRIAN smiles, PAPO smirks and looks away. BRIAN starts to walk away.)

PAPO: What's the matter, man? You don't say hello?

BRIAN: I thought you were mad at me.

PAPO: I should be.

BRIAN: I've been looking for you.

PAPO: You can't have been looking too hard. I'm always right here.

BRIAN: You're not wearing the sweater.

PAPO: Yeah, well, I don't wear it everyday, you know. I gotta give it a rest.

BRIAN: So, how are you doing?

PAPO: Look, are you buying or what?

BRIAN: I just wanted to see you, to talk. I thought you might be happy to see me.

PAPO: Well I ain't.

(BRIAN looks down at PAPO's crotch.)

BRIAN: I think you are.

PAPO: That's not fair, man. I don't wear underwears.

BRIAN: I just wanted to say I'm sorry about the other day.

PAPO: *(Shrugs)* Fuck it.

(BRIAN turns to enter peep show.)

PAPO: Hey, where the fuck are you going? Hot damn. You come all the way down here to apologize and then you go try to pick up somebody else.

BRIAN: Sssh. I thought you were still mad at me.

PAPO: I fucking should be.

BRIAN: Would you like to go to dinner?

PAPO: Time is money.

BRIAN: Can you take some time off?

PAPO: What you think, I punch a fucking time clock?

BRIAN: You got such a mouth on you.

PAPO: Yeah, good lips, huh?

BRIAN: Do I have to pay you to take you to dinner?

PAPO: Hey, don't stand in front of me, you're blocking my fucking view.

(When BRIAN shifts he begins to stare at somebody else.)

PAPO: You know, it's not like I ain't got other mother fuckers waiting for me. You fucking show up out of nowheres and—

(PAPO notices BRIAN staring at someone else. He slaps the back of his head.)

PAPO: Hey, mother fucker, you planning on taking the whole fucking deuce to dinner?

BRIAN: No, just you. If you'll come.

PAPO: Like if I'm gonna turn down free food.

BRIAN: Do you want to go home and change?

PAPO: No, do you?

(Blackout. Lights up on restaurant. PAPO *and* BRIAN *seated at a small round table. Very nice place—linen tablecloth and napkins. In the background* BOBBY *is softly lit. He sits on the bed, smoking, waiting for* PAPO. *He remains seated throughout the scene.)*

PAPO: Is this how you white people eat every day. *(He touches tablecloth and napkins.)* Look, it's all material.

BRIAN: Lower your voice.

PAPO: *(In a basso profundo)* It's all material.

*(*BRIAN *laughs.)*

PAPO: Seriously, how much does it cost to eat here?

BRIAN: It's my treat. Don't worry about it.

PAPO: The waiter looked at me like I belonged 'cause I came in with you. Hey, where's my napkin holder? You got one of them glass napkin rings. Where's mine?

BRIAN: Here, you can have mine.

PAPO: No, I'll just take one of the little mother fuckers off another table.

BRIAN: Papo, don't.

PAPO: They ain't in use.

BRIAN: Take mine.

*(*PAPO *gets up and returns with one.)*

PAPO: Ta-da.

BRIAN: Sssh.

PAPO: Am I embarrassing you, faggot?

*(*BRIAN *looks away.* PAPO *sits.)*

PAPO: Look man, I'm sorry. Really. I won't call you that again. I swears.

BRIAN: Just tell me what you want from the menu.

PAPO: Now you're mad at me.

BRIAN: No, I'm not.

PAPO: Don't fucking be that way.

BRIAN: *(Sharply)* Can you talk without cursing?

PAPO: When did I fucking curse?

BRIAN: You don't even hear it anymore.

PAPO: I hear what I want to hear. You should try it sometime.

BRIAN: You mean some fucking time.

PAPO: That ain't cursing.

BRIAN: Fuck is a verb, not an adjective.

PAPO: Fool, if anybody knows that I do.

BRIAN: Let's make a deal. Let's see if we can have a nice meal with no cursing.

PAPO: Seriously, man, I don't call that cursing. Cursing is when I'm mad at somebody. Like when I "used" to call you faggot. I used that as a curse.

BRIAN: Could you also try to speak a little softer?

PAPO: Maybe if that guy could hold off on the piano for a bit. *(Calls to piano player)* Hey, man.

BRIAN: Papo. Shut up. Now.

*(*PAPO *stares at* BRIAN *a second, then smiles.)*

PAPO: You getting all butch on me all of a sudden?

BRIAN: Maybe this wasn't such a good idea.

PAPO: I'll be good. Look, I won't say another word. So, what do you do?

BRIAN: I'm a lawyer.

PAPO: Fucking judge must go crazy when he sees you.

BRIAN: Papo.

PAPO: Right.

BRIAN: I've been in New York a little over a year. Just bought a co-op.

PAPO: Nice, nice.

BRIAN: Pretty much a stay-to-myself type. I'm very discreet. Don't have too many gay friends.

PAPO: I ain't gay.

BRIAN: Okay.

PAPO: I'm not.

BRIAN: Fine.

PAPO: When did you know you were a fag...uh, a queer?

BRIAN: Do you care?

*(*PAPO *shrugs.)*

BRIAN: I always knew it. Sometimes I feel like I'm going to die if I can't have sex; then other times I think I'll die if I do have it.

PAPO: Man, you is how old and you're still a virgin?

*(*BRIAN *sees waiter. He elbows* PAPO.*)*

BRIAN: I'll have the house salad with vinaigrette dressing, onion soup, and duck in raspberry sauce.

PAPO: Me, too.

(Waiter disappears. BRIAN *takes a drink of water.)*

PAPO: So when can I pop your cherry?

*(*BRIAN *chokes on water.)*

PAPO: Hey man, I don't mean right here.

BRIAN: Let's just see if we can make it through this dinner without you giving me a heart attack. Okay?

PAPO: Yeah, okay. I have that effect on people sometimes.

BRIAN: Making them choke?

PAPO: *(Sly smile)* That too.

BRIAN: Uh, do you have any family here?

PAPO: I don't wanna talk about them.

BRIAN: Okay.

PAPO: Do you like talking about your parents?

BRIAN: I said okay.

(Pause)

PAPO: What do you talk about when you're with your white friends?

BRIAN: What do you mean?

PAPO: I'm no dummy. Talk English to me and I'll understand you.

BRIAN: I don't think you're stupid.

PAPO: Yeah, well, you fucking better not. Talk to me.

BRIAN: Okay, how old are you?

PAPO: Jesus fucking Christ!

BRIAN: Lower your voice.

PAPO: I'm surprised you got any fucking friends. I'm not as old as I look.

BRIAN: I just wanted to know how long you've been at it.

PAPO: You mean fucking fags?

*(*BRIAN *tenses.* PAPO *puts his hand on* BRIAN*'s arm and mouths "Sorry.")*

BRIAN: This is not working.

PAPO: Sure it is, just fucking relax.

BRIAN: You get angry at everything I say.

PAPO: No I don't. I started at fifteen.

BRIAN: Why?

PAPO: I don't know. I was a real delicacy then. Flavor of the month. The last Coca-Cola in the desert. I made a lot of money.

BRIAN: What's a lot of money?

PAPO: I once made three hundred dollars in one day.

*(*BRIAN *whistles appreciatively.* PAPO *smiles.)*

BRIAN: That is a lot of money.

PAPO: I gave most of it to my parents. They bought a new living room set.

BRIAN: What did you have to do to earn it?

*(*PAPO *gives* BRIAN *a dirty look.)*

BRIAN: Sorry.

PAPO: Most people think that all Puerto Ricans are strung-out hustlers. I read, you know. I do fucking crossword puzzles. I don't do drugs. You don't have to be embarrassed by me. I'm not stupid.

BRIAN: I never said you were stupid.

PAPO: You like me, right?

BRIAN: Yeah.

PAPO: Then talk to me. Trust me, I'll understand you.

BRIAN: What do you want me to say?

PAPO: You're a lawyer. Why did you become a lawyer?

BRIAN: To make money.

PAPO: See? We got things in common.

*(*BRIAN *laughs.)*

BRIAN: I put myself through law school. I almost had to drop out twice.

PAPO: Why?

BRIAN: Money.

PAPO: I thought all white people had money.

BRIAN: We don't. I once had to carry two jobs and keep my grades up.

PAPO: Shit.

BRIAN: Now I've got a good job and I make good money.

PAPO: Yeah?

BRIAN: I'm not rich, but I can buy things for myself now and then. Pamper myself. Take friends to dinner.

(PAPO smiles.)

BRIAN: Things I read about but could never afford to do.

(PAPO's hand begins to fondle BRIAN under the table.)

BRIAN: Don't do that.

(PAPO continues.)

PAPO: *(Teasing)* Why not? You no like?

BRIAN: Please put your hands on top of the table.

PAPO: Lower your voice.

(BRIAN reaches under the table to remove PAPO's hand.)

PAPO: It looks even worse with both of our hands under here.

(BRIAN whips his hand out. PAPO continues groping.)

PAPO: This is better.

BRIAN: Please stop.

PAPO: No one can see us. Relax. Drink a little fucking water. You feel real healthy down here.

BRIAN: The waiter is coming.

PAPO: Tell him to go the fuck away.

BRIAN: We're not quite ready yet.

(PAPO continues groping.)

BRIAN: Please, this is enough. Stop it.

PAPO: Take me back to your place?

(BRIAN shakes his head "No.")

BRIAN: *(Whispers)* Yes.

PAPO: Do you have any fantasy you want to live out?

BRIAN: I just don't want to die.

(PAPO freezes.)

PAPO: Do you really want me to stop?

BRIAN: If you stop I'll die.

(Blackout. BOBBY *hears a noise in the hallway and hurriedly puts out the cigarette. He opens the window and tries to air the room by waving his hands. He is stopped by the silence in the hallway. He listens by the door. He is about to relight his cigarette again, but stops. He gently drops the cigarette out the window. He waves goodbye to it as it falls. Lights fade out on* BOBBY.*)*

(Lights up on BRIAN, *who is asleep among his sheets.* PAPO *enters. He carries a supermarket bag and places it on the floor. He exits and returns, wheeling a portable T V set, and positions it in front of the bed. He is carrying the remote control for it in his mouth. He exits again and returns with two plates, two spoons, and a knife. He puts the plates on the bed, trying to be as quiet as possible so as not to awaken* BRIAN. PAPO'*s mood is very up. He takes a pint of ice cream and a pound cake from the bag. He cuts the cake in half, putting a half on each plate. He opens the ice cream and divides it the same way. He puts the knife aside, puts the ice cream container in the bag, and then quickly, but quietly, strips. He gently gets into bed and puts both plates on his lap. He aims the remote control at the T V. Loud cartoon music is heard.* BRIAN *jumps up.)*

PAPO: Good morning.

BRIAN: What the hell? Lower that goddamn thing!

PAPO: Shit. And you talk about my mother fucking mouth.

BRIAN: What's going on here?

PAPO: I made breakfast in bed. Here.

*(*PAPO *hands* BRIAN *a plate.)*

PAPO: And they're doing Bugs Bunny. The old ones.

BRIAN: Could you lower that a little?

PAPO: Man, if I put it any lower I won't be able to fucking hear it. *(He lowers the volume.)* You got a real problem with sound, you know that?

*(*BRIAN *lays back and watches* PAPO, *who is lost in his cartoons.)*

BRIAN: I've got to take a shower.

PAPO: You've had three since we got here. *(He continues eating. He watches the cartoons and reacts to them. He takes* BRIAN'*s hand with his free hand.)* You still think God is gonna strike you dead?

BRIAN: What?

*(*PAPO *laughs at the cartoon.)*

PAPO: What's up doc?

BRIAN: I have to go to work.

(PAPO tries to kiss him with his mouth full of ice cream. BRIAN turns his head.)

PAPO: Time for a quickie?

(BRIAN jumps from the bed and pulls the sheet around him.)

BRIAN: Do you want to, uh, do you want to take a shower first?

(PAPO takes the remote and ups the volume. BRIAN takes it from him and shuts off the T V. PAPO studies his ice cream.)

BRIAN: I don't want to be late.

PAPO: I guess you're done with this spic, huh?

(BRIAN gets his wallet and places it gently on the bed next to PAPO.)

BRIAN: Papo, I am petrified of you. *(He tries to smooth PAPO's head but PAPO violently shakes him off.)*

PAPO: So you kicking me out, right? *(Silence)* Are you kicking me out?

BRIAN: Yes.

(PAPO puts his plate on the bed and gets dressed. He begins to put on a shoe.)

BRIAN: Will you please take some money from me?

(Without looking up, PAPO throws the shoe at BRIAN. PAPO gets himself under control and puts on his other shoe. BRIAN brings the shoe to him and stands by PAPO with it in his hand. PAPO takes it and puts it on. He never looks up at BRIAN. When PAPO stands he punches BRIAN in the stomach. BRIAN doubles over as PAPO exits.)

(Flophouse. BOBBY is sleeping while hugging a pillow. PAPO enters. He stares at BOBBY and quietly walks to the bed where he gently kisses BOBBY, who continues sleeping. PAPO goes to the hot plate and takes a sauce pan from it. He uncovers it and begins to eat Rice-a-roni directly from it. He sits on the bed, next to BOBBY, who slowly wakes up.)

PAPO: Hey, Baby.

(BOBBY shimmies up to PAPO and lays his head in his lap.)

PAPO: Got a little lost looking for the cake.

BOBBY: Sssh. How'd it go, Reggie?

PAPO: Not too good, Baby. A lot of distractions. Didn't get jackshit done. Just ran around with my finger up my ass.

(BOBBY giggles. PAPO begins to feed him like a baby. Tenderly, playfully:)

PAPO: You keeping out of mischief?

BOBBY: Uh-huh.

PAPO: Good boy.

BOBBY: Gimme a kiss, Reggie.

(A knock is heard.)

PAPO: *(To door)* Hold on a second.

*(*PAPO *gives* BOBBY *a kiss.* BOBBY *throws his arms around* PAPO*'s neck.* PAPO *must pull him off.)*

PAPO: Look Baby, that's the man from downstairs and he wants his rent.

BOBBY: Ronald.

PAPO: Right. Look, I bullshitted the night away and we has got to pay the rent.

BOBBY: Don't let him in.

*(*PAPO *kisses* BOBBY *on the shoulder.)*

PAPO: Baby, he's just gonna touch you a little, that's all.

(Another knock is heard. PAPO *yells to door.)*

PAPO: Hey fucking dickhead, fucking chill out for a second. *(He goes to door and opens it. Doorway light comes into room.)* You all fucking ready and set to explode?

*(*PAPO *pulls the sheet off* BOBBY, *who is face down and eating from the pan. A whistle from the man is heard.)*

PAPO: Good, huh?

*(*PAPO *motions for the man to enter and he turns to leave.* BOBBY *reaches out and takes* PAPO*'s hand.)*

BOBBY: Okay, but you stay. You stay. You promise.

(The lights from the doorway and the room begin to dim. BOBBY *closes his eyes and squeezes* PAPO*'s hand.)*

BOBBY: This is for you.

(Blackout)

PAPO: With one guy I'm an open sore. The one thing I am I can't be with him. I'm good at sex, real good, but I can't do it with him because it makes him nervous. Hey, but wait a second, lemme rewind my past and I'll erase it. I'll be nice and clean for the big white hunter. And I still won't be good enough for him. But I can go to nice places with him, I can go to stores and not have store detectives follow me as if I were gonna steal something. He's one of them and if I'm with him I must be okay, too. White by marriage. Which with Baby would be pretty useless. I mean, to be white and poor I might as well stay the way I fucking am. Then you start falling in love. You know, the stupid stuff. What kind of guy falls in love with another guy? With two other guys? Yeah, 'cause once you start with that shit it takes on a fucking life of its own. My life.

(Night. PAPO *enters phone booth. Lights up on* BRIAN, *in bathrobe, in his bedroom.* BRIAN*'s phone rings.)*

PAPO: Hi, Brian, this is Papo.

BRIAN: Ah, listen, I'm about getting ready to leave.

PAPO: Yeah, where to?

BRIAN: I'm meeting some friends for dinner.

PAPO: So you wanna hang out later?

BRIAN: We'll be out late.

PAPO: That's okay.

BRIAN: I don't think so.

PAPO: C'mon man. Fuck, if you're just half as horny as I am we'll set the sheets on fire.

*(*BRIAN *hangs up.* PAPO *is left holding a dead receiver. He starts to hit the phone with the receiver. He fishes into his pocket for another quarter and calls* BRIAN.*)*

BRIAN: Papo, please.

PAPO: Don't you ever, ever fucking hang up on me.

*(*BRIAN *hangs up.* PAPO *inserts another quarter while hitting the phone booth in a rage. He yells at someone waiting to use the phone.)*

PAPO: I ain't fucking finished yet. You wanna do something about it, huh? Wait your goddamn turn, cunt.

*(*PAPO *flails with one hand at someone waiting for the phone while dialing with the other hand. The phone rings and rings.)*

PAPO: Please pick up.

*(*BRIAN *finally picks up.)*

BRIAN: Papo.

PAPO: Do you want me to go over there, is that it? Do you want me to show up where you work? I will, you know I will. Don't fuck with me, Brian.

(Pause)

BRIAN: What do you want from me?

PAPO: Why can't I see you?

BRIAN: Papo.

PAPO: I ain't so fucking bad. And you like me, I know you do.

BRIAN: Look, Papo... Okay, I'll meet you at the Peep Show in twenty minutes.

PAPO: I'm right outside your apartment. I'm calling from the corner.

BRIAN: You're what?!

PAPO: Don't get mad, man. I'm just hanging out.

BRIAN: Are you spying on me?

PAPO: No, no, I swear.

BRIAN: Walk away from my building. I'll meet you at Thirty-fourth and Fifth in ten minutes.

PAPO: Yeah, okay.

BRIAN: If I see you at the phone booth when I leave the building I'll turn around and go right back in.

PAPO: And I'll fucking crack your head in. *(Pause)* Thirty-fourth and Fifth.

BRIAN: Thirty-fourth and Fifth.

PAPO: Well, fucking hurry up.

*(*BRIAN *hangs up.)*

PAPO: 'Cause I miss you.

(Thirty-fourth and Fifth. PAPO *is wearing* BRIAN*'s sweater. Enter* BRIAN.*)*

PAPO: Yo man, fancy meeting you here.

BRIAN: Hi, Papo.

PAPO: Check out the sweater, man. I'm wearing the sweater you bought for me.

BRIAN: What do you want?

PAPO: Hey, just a little action. That's all.

(He playfully grabs BRIAN *who moves away.)*

BRIAN: Are you crazy? This is not the Peep Show.

PAPO: Oh yeah, I forgot. Decent people hang out here.

BRIAN: That's not it.

PAPO: People who never have sex.

BRIAN: Look, I've got to get up early tomorrow.

PAPO: So what? You were gonna meet your white friends for dinner, weren't you?

BRIAN: They're friends, period. And I called and canceled.

PAPO: Shit. You weren't gonna meet nobody. You were probably at home playing with your meat when I called.

(BRIAN starts to walk away, PAPO follows.)

PAPO: Let's go back to your place.

BRIAN: I don't ever want you in my home again.

PAPO: And have a little party. Take one of the side streets, there are less people there.

(On a dimmer street. PAPO grabs BRIAN and kisses him.)

BRIAN: This has got to stop.

PAPO: Okay.

BRIAN: I mean it. Don't call me, don't follow me.

PAPO: Fine. Don't desire me.

BRIAN: Your ego, like your brain, is in your crotch.

PAPO: No man, I don't think so.

BRIAN: You don't think, period.

PAPO: 'Cause I ain't the only one doing the following.

BRIAN: You're crazy.

PAPO: And I ain't the one who checked out the meat the first chance I got.

(BRIAN turns to leave; PAPO grabs his arm.)

PAPO: I get my rocks off seven times a day. How do you do?

(PAPO slowly pulls BRIAN toward him.)

PAPO: I don't think you do too well. I think you probably got a real tired hand.

BRIAN: I can't. Please. I just want to go back to the way it was—

PAPO: The only trouble with being alone is there's no one there to kiss back.

BRIAN: —before I met you.

(PAPO holds BRIAN and kisses him.)

PAPO: Now you kiss me.

BRIAN: I can't.

PAPO: I'm not gonna fucking move. You kiss me.

(They stare at each other. BRIAN slowly moves toward PAPO.)

PAPO: Keep your eyes open. I want you to see who you're kissing.

(BRIAN kisses PAPO. The kiss builds in passion until PAPO breaks free.)

PAPO: No, you don't wanna see me. Tell me you don't wanna see me.

BRIAN: *(In a small voice)* I don't want to see you.

PAPO: You know, you're really full of shit, man. You'd rather be home jerking off by yourself. Is that it?

BRIAN: No.

(PAPO kisses him.)

PAPO: Is that it?

BRIAN: *(Whispers)* No.

PAPO: No what?

BRIAN: Don't go.

PAPO: Why not?

BRIAN: Please.

PAPO: Are you horny? *(Silence)* Let me hear you say it, man. Are you horny?

BRIAN: I'm horny.

(PAPO puts his arms around BRIAN.)

PAPO: What do you want me to do about it? Put your arms around my neck.

BRIAN: We're in the middle of the street.

PAPO: It's dark, man.

(BRIAN does.)

PAPO: Maybe I can help you do what you do alone.

BRIAN: Yes, please.

PAPO: But where? You told me you don't want me in your home. I'm too dirty for your home, right?

(PAPO kisses BRIAN as they embrace. A car goes by; someone yells "Faggot." BRIAN tries to break free. PAPO holds him. BRIAN stops struggling and they kiss again.)

PAPO: I'll see you around, Brian. *(He begins to walk away.)* Have to go back to where I belong. Got a nice, seventeen-year-old white boy waiting up for me. You better hurry home, too. You don't want to keep your hand waiting.

(BRIAN follows PAPO and begins to hit him. PAPO tries to hold his hands and they begin to fight. PAPO wraps his arms around BRIAN, pinning his arms down.)

PAPO: Say it.

BRIAN: Fuck you.

PAPO: Say it or I walk.

(Pause)

BRIAN: Please come home with me.

*(*PAPO *lets* BRIAN *go.)*

PAPO: Why?

BRIAN: 'Cause I want you.

PAPO: How much do you want me?

BRIAN: I want you.

PAPO: I don't believe you.

BRIAN: I want you.

PAPO: I still don't believe you.

*(*BRIAN *gets on his knees.)*

BRIAN: I want you.

*(*PAPO *kneels with* BRIAN. *They embrace.)*

(Blackout)

(Flophouse)

BOBBY: Please don't go, please don't go, please don't go.

PAPO: This is my last chance. I ain't no sweet-looking little kid anymore. I've got mileage on me and it's beginning to show.

BOBBY: You got somebody else.

PAPO: Yeah.

BOBBY: I love you, Reggie.

PAPO: Well, he loves me too. And he knows my name.

BOBBY: Do you like him better than you like me?

PAPO: I must.

BOBBY: He's never gonna love you like I love you.

PAPO: I didn't have to come back here to tell you, you know. What the hell do I have here that I have to take with me?

BOBBY: You mean besides my heart?

*(*PAPO *hits* BOBBY.*)*

BOBBY: I don't want to fight with you, Reggie.

PAPO: C'mon Shithead. You fucking pissed off, right? Go ahead, hit me. Hit me.

*(*PAPO *continues to jab at* BOBBY, *who grabs* PAPO*'s hand and kisses it.)*

BOBBY: I love you.

*(*PAPO *pushes him away.)*

PAPO: Cut the fucking shit. You love Reggie, not me. What the fuck am I supposed to do, turn tricks until we're old and gray?

BOBBY: I'm yours, Papo. I'm your Baby.

PAPO: I never asked for you, you fucking fruitcake.

*(*BOBBY *reaches between the mattress and box spring and pulls out his knife. He tries to stab himself.* PAPO *wrests the knife from him. He sits on the floor, cradling* BOBBY.*)*

BOBBY: Oh please don't go. Please.

PAPO: Sssh, sssh. Ronald's a good guy. He loves you too, Baby.

BOBBY: You're the one for me.

PAPO: No, I'm the one for me, period. *(He gets up, takes the knife, and heads to the door.)* You'll be okay, guy. You're probably right. Nobody's gonna love me like you do. Even if you don't know who I am.

BOBBY: I don't know who you are? I don't know who you fucking are?! I can be you, anybody can be you. What's so fucking tough about pushing people away? But can you be me? Come on, Papo, can you be me? Can you love anybody the way I love you? I know who you are. I love you.

PAPO: Get the fuck outta my face.

BOBBY: I know who you are. I love you, Papo.

PAPO: And you call me by somebody else's name?

BOBBY: Would it have made any difference if I called you Papo?

*(*PAPO *exits.)*

BOBBY: When did I stop being your Baby? *(He goes to window. Lights dim as he opens it.)*

(Lights up on street. PAPO *enters and begins to walk. A siren approaches and crowd voices are heard.)*

VOICE 1: What happened?

VOICE 2: Some little white boy in panties jumped out the window.

VOICE 1: I think he's dead.

VOICE 3: One less faggot.

*(*PAPO *pauses, staring straight ahead. After a few beats he continues walking, totally expressionless. He slowly begins to shake. He runs toward the flophouse and cradles* BOBBY*'s body.)*

PAPO: It'll be okay, Baby. You're my baby and I'm here. I'm right here.

(The music from the beginning of the play starts, with the voices and the sirens. PAPO *rocks* BOBBY*'s body. He removes sweater [the one* BRIAN *gave him] and wraps it around* BOBBY*. He continues to rock him as the music, voices, and lights begin to dim.)*

PAPO: Bring back my heart, you little mother fucker.

END OF PLAY